THE
FUN
OF DYING

FIND OUT WHAT REALLY HAPPENS NEXT!

ROBERTA GRIMES

THE FUN OF DYING

Contact:
Greater Reality Publications
http://greaterreality.com
800 827-3770
E-mail: info@greaterreality.com
Order copies: http://orders.greaterreality.com

Contact the Author:
www.FunofDying.com

ISBN 978-0-9802111-1-5

Book Design by Ricky G. Russ Jr. | www.r1cky.com

Contents

*This book is lovingly dedicated
to each of the thousands of researchers
whose diligent work made it possible.*

# INTRODUCTION

I had an experience of light at the age of eight and spent the next half-century figuring it out. I tell you this only to explain why I have lived my life obsessed with death. It has been an odd hobby, but a thrilling one. By studying death, eventually I was able to explain my experience of light, but that turned out to be a side-adventure. In the process of reading hundreds of books, many of them long out of print, I came to understand the death process and its aftermath well enough to write a travelogue. I learned how death happens, how it feels, what comes next, and so much more about how reality works that I am more obsessed with death now than I ever was.

I didn't set out to write this whole book. What I wanted to write was Chapters 6 through 8, set in large print and illustrated, something to give to dying people to help ease their fears and better prepare them for what is life's most enjoyable adventure. I soon found, though, that to write for the dying and make it even remotely believable I had to tackle the rest of this book.

It's a big story! A century and a half of detailed and consistent evidence makes it easy to piece together how death happens and why for most of us, it is the best time of our lives. Not only is the evidence consistent with quantum physics and many religions, but it makes sense. When suddenly I understood that, the realization felt like curing cancer, achieving world peace, and discovering the meaning of life all at once. Knowing the truth about death changes everything.

Although others have undertaken similar research and reached more or less the same conclusions, there are reasons why so few have written about the death event. Evidence is widely available, but it isn't easy to pull together. And to talk about dying with authority is to set oneself against those two modern bastions, mainstream science and mainstream religion, which long ago carved up all truth between them and thereby have shut out any facts that neither of them wants to own.

Then too, there is the credentials problem. I am an attorney by profession so I am a hobbyist and not a careerist, and there are many professional scholars who could have done a better job of writing this book. The problem is, however, that nearly all researchers have chosen some tiny, compelling part of what is an enormous picture and made a career of it, each of them trying to gain some attention without drawing ridicule. After all, if you have academic credentials and if near-death experiences or past-life memories or the accuracy of mediums or the zero-point field is your area, then what you hope for is recognition. What you never want is scorn.

Sadly, though, scorn is what these researchers earn, and there are some good reasons for that which you will shortly understand. But knowing that even this field's greatest scholars have been ignored by the scientific community, I have not attempted here to make a scientific case. Instead, I am making my case to you, and using to make it the general tools that you use in your daily life and work: reason, deduction, and common sense. I am not writing for scientists. I only note in passing that for scientific gatekeepers to continue to enforce atheism as a fundamental dogma is as counterproductive now as it once was for scientists stuck in Catholic orthodoxy to insist against evidence that the earth was flat. Truth cannot be suppressed forever, so the academic dam is certain to break. And when it does, the revelations soon to follow about who and what and where we are will change all humanity for the better.

It isn't only scientific oxen that we will be goring here, but some religious folks will be incensed. I am sorry about that. If you prefer to believe whatever it is that your own religion teaches, all I ask is that you be open-minded whenever your own death starts to happen. As you will see, one way to give yourself unnecessary grief is to insist on a certain kind of afterlife. But otherwise, the good news is that the afterlife is not a guessing-game. Catholics and Baptists both get into heaven. And Jews and Buddhists. And everybody else.

I have tried to pare the results of decades of research into a book so brief and so easy to read that most people will enjoy it. I have avoided footnotes because most of what is said here is supported by so many sources that to cite just a few seemed problematic. Then too, most of my research was done long before it occurred to me to write a book. So instead of presenting footnotes, I have assembled a pair of study guides in Appendix I to help you learn these truths for yourself. You will find there some of my favorite books, and many of them contain bibliographies, so if you wind up sharing my interest you can spend the rest of your life reading.

The first chapter of this book surveys the available afterlife evidence and tackles some of the problems that are inherent in doing this research. Chapters 2–5 tie the afterlife evidence to the reality that we think we see, since for many of us the evidence seems too far-fetched unless we understand how it might fit with what we know. Chapters 6–9 discuss the dying process and what happens to us soon after death, so if you don't share my difficulty with believing what you cannot see, then feel free to go right to Chapter 6.

This book's title may have made you wince, but the word "fun" had to be there because variants of it are so often used by the dead to summarize their dying experiences and the places where they arrived. They don't speak of the afterlife in religious terms. Instead, in countless ways they tell us that, quite unexpectedly, being dead has turned out to be a whole lot of fun.

(I should add, though, that death by suicide is the opposite of fun. If you have opened this book because you are contemplating hastening your own demise, please skip ahead and read Chapter 9. Then figure out how to get back to living.)

It is time now – it is long past time – to talk about death as the adventure that it is. Learn the truth for yourself and tell everyone you know. With 160,000 people dying daily, it is tragic that in the 21st century so many still die in ignorance and fear.

CHAPTER ONE

WHY IS THE TRUTH ABOUT DEATH NOT COMMON KNOWLEDGE?

*"Misguided interpretations of quantum physics
are a classic hallmark of pseudoscience ... Authors
with religious motives make shameless appeals
to common sense...."*
Opinion section editor of *New Scientist*, 28 February, 2009

*"Ask and it will be given to you; seek and you will find;
knock and the door will be opened to you. For everyone
who asks receives; he who seeks finds; and to him
who knocks, the door will be opened."*
Yeshua (better known as Jesus) (MT 7:7-8)

*M*ost of the facts are known about what happens when we die. But very few scientists work in this field, and those who do are ignored (or worse). So for most people, this universal trip still is as scary as sailing used to be when the flat earth had edges and the sea was full of dragons.

How is it possible that the truth about death has been so well hidden for so long? Two factors are involved, I think:

- Until the last decade, not enough information was widely enough available to allow us to achieve a reasonable understanding. Many of the important facts have been known for a century or more. But until some recent breakthroughs filled in a few crucial gaps, it was hard to make sense of the whole picture.

- For the last two thousand years, nearly the history of civilization, people have chosen to divide human knowledge into two jealously competing camps, one material and one spiritual. Since modern evidence tells us that the truth about reality lies somewhere between, we can expect that neither scientists nor clergymen will take the lead in doing afterlife research. Knowledge of what happens at death is going to be a grassroots breakthrough, spreading from person to person rather than coming down from experts.

Terminology

You will notice that throughout this book I refer to the end-of-life transition as "death," and to people who have transitioned as "dead people." I do this deliberately. In fact, the change that we call death is a passage as easy as a sneeze into a reality far happier and even more alive than this one is, so it is past time for us to stop being afraid to use the word. At worst, death is a brief illusion of separation from some of those we love; at best, it is a glorious new freedom. But it is not in any sense an ending. So let's use the word. It is time to stop fearing it.

Religion vs. Science vs. Religion vs. Science…

Let's talk briefly about science and religion, not to dismiss them but rather to understand why neither has taken the lead in this research. After all, as one physicist told me, whoever proves that there is life after death is going to win a Nobel Prize, so if there were anything to it, there would be scientists working on it now; and as one clergyman said to me firmly, there is no need to investigate the afterlife when the Lord Jesus Christ said it all. Mainstream scientists believe that there is nothing after death to discover, while mainstream clergymen are sure that there is nothing more to know.

Mainstream Science

Physics is the core science on which the other scientific disciplines are based, and until about a hundred years ago it made steady and impressive progress. Then early in the 20th century physics more or less ran off the rails when its two fundamental concepts – Newtonian physics, which works on large objects; and quantum physics, which works at the subatomic level – were found to be incompatible. To vastly simplify what is a big problem, since both Newtonian and quantum physics are well-proven theories in their own domains, physicists have spent the past century searching with an ever-increasing sense of frustration for a theory of physics that encompasses them both. But perhaps such a unified theory won't be found, because (as you will shortly see) the very matter and energy and time and space that physicists are trying to understand do not exist in most of reality. In a sense, you might say that they don't exist at all.

Many scientists believe in God, but mainstream science's dogmas and protocols have long been fundamentally atheistic. In that, modern science has become a belief-system not unlike a religion. Like other belief-systems it has its gatekeepers in place to enforce its orthodoxies: its peer-reviewed journals, its university departments, its institutes, and its grants-giving foundations. Together these gatekeepers have ensured that no whiff of any theory that smacks of the existence of God has ever found scientific acceptance.

At one time atheism may have been useful in protecting science from religious interference, but now it has become an impediment. What quantum physicists have found is the place where the material meets the non-material, and until enough of them come to terms with that fact, they will never venture far enough to see what apparently underlies everything.

Mainstream Religions

Religions are belief-systems. They are based upon faith and not upon facts; or, more precisely, they are based upon modern faith in a set of ancient facts. There is no room in most religious denominations for any new information, in part because each denomination fights so hard to protect its own cherished doctrines. Recall that old joke about Catholics and Baptists living in separate rooms in heaven (since each group thinks that the other is in hell), and you realize how much each denomination has invested in enforcing its own beliefs.

Some of the Eastern religions have for millennia held theories about death which have turned out to be pretty close to what evidence now tells us is true. But mainstream Christianity has not shared the Easterners' curiosity about details. Instead, it has set up a generic heaven as a reward for having followed the rules, and a generic hell as the ultimate cudgel to keep the faithful from leaving the flock. So while Christians believe in an afterlife, our mental picture of life after death is full of clouds and thrones and hell and fire and the terror of God's judgment. Even believing that a heaven exists seems to do little to ease our fear of death.

Our Need to Open Our Minds

Dividing human knowledge into material and spiritual truths may have made sense in Plato's day, but today it makes no sense at all. Truth can defend itself against error, and if it cannot do that then it is not truth. For centuries, misguided attempts to protect outmoded truths have been a primary obstacle to the advancement of our knowledge. If no one had questioned the settled science that balancing bodily humors improved health or that each sperm contained a tiny human being or that the flat earth was the center of the universe, then our understanding of what is true would have advanced little in a thousand years. When you study 150 years worth of long-ignored evidence of our eternal life, you realize how much harm has been done by our segregating two kinds of truth and ignoring whatever fit nobody's dogmas, which is why we won't be doing that here. Instead, we will take the opposite approach, and use both scientific and religious facts to validate and further reinforce what afterlife evidence now tells us. This approach may seem odd to you at first, but remember that what we are seeking here is neither scientific nor religious truth, but rather human truth without either bias.

Overcoming Our Belief-Based Anxieties

Anyone who wants to understand what actually happens when we die is not going to get much help from either mainstream science or mainstream religions. That turns out not to be much of a problem, since for the past century there have been quiet researchers of every stripe working to document what has turned out to be a lot of evidence. Their lives' work is all there for the studying. To do that, however, we religious types first have to make a logical leap, and accept the fact that – no matter what our religious leaders say – no religion owns God.

Religious anxieties have been my biggest problem. Even as I spent decades in research, for most of that time I rejected anything that seemed to be inconsistent with Christianity. For years I felt stymied, still firmly Christian but ever more certain that the evidence was right, and – like any modern-day physicist – unable to reconcile the two. Then finally it occurred to me to sit down and read only the Gospels.

For those not familiar with the Bible, the Gospels are four accounts of the life of Jesus. They begin the New Testament, the rest of which is commentary by the Apostle Paul and others. The Gospels are the only place where the words of Jesus are reported, and I found that reading just his words without Paul's earnest interpretations was a revelation. I have included here some of the results of my Gospel study, even though my doing so may annoy both religious and non-religious readers. However:

- If you are *a Christian*, consider that besides whatever you understand to be the greater import of the life of Jesus, his words are consistent with modern evidence for an afterlife. This makes him all the more remarkable.

- If you are *not a Christian*, think how affirming it is that the words of someone who lived long ago and claimed to know the truth about death are entirely consistent with evidence that first came to light two thousand years later.

In an attempt to mollify both camps, I will here refer to Jesus by his Aramaic name, and I won't capitalize his pronouns.

It was Yeshua who sealed the deal for me. Having first done decades of research, I was astonished to read the Gospels freshly and realize that the recorded words of Yeshua are consistent in even small details with modern evidence of what happens when we die. This unexpected validation seems to me quite amazing and wonderful. It would be inexcusable not to share it.

I should add, though, that nothing said here is based on the teachings of any religion. Everything mentioned in this book appears in lay sources; and except where noted otherwise, each detail can be found repeatedly. The Gospel words of Yeshua are used here only because they support and further illuminate the modern evidence. To tip into scientific lingo for a moment, what are the odds against chance of that?

The Evidence

The scientific method serves us well, but it cannot be used to study life after death. Most replicable experiments are impossible, mathematics appears to be irrelevant, and much of what we know about material reality does not seem to apply beyond death. So we will approach the study of what happens at death in a different way, by looking for consistencies in a century and a half of varied evidence.

Most of the evidence of what happens at death is personal to one or to just a few people, so it goes without saying that no single story – and no group of stories – can be considered trustworthy. However, when hundreds of such stories are studied as a whole, many detailed common experiences emerge. Here are some of the kinds of evidence that we will be using in the chapters that follow:

- **Deathbed Visions.** Before the middle of the 20th century, most people died at home, unsedated. It was then widely observed that dying people would be visited by departed loved ones who had come to ease their passage. Recorded accounts by bedside witnesses are stunningly consistent and highly evidentiary. It is obvious that these dying people experienced something that they thought was real.

- **Near-Death Experiences.** Reported deathbed visions are less common now because most of the dying are sedated, but near-death experiences happen more frequently as people whose bodies have been technically dead are revived through the efforts of modern medicine. These people often tell amaz-ing stories. No two near-death experiences are alike, but the death process and the after-death reality that they show us are remarkably consistent across the genre.

- **Communications Through Psychic Mediums.** My research with mediums has convinced me that many of them rely on our cues and some may be outright charlatans. But this is one area where double- and triple-blind scientific studies are possible, and these studies suggest that some psychic mediums are indeed in contact with the dead.

- **Communications Through Deep-Trance Mediums.** Unlike the mind-contact with dead Aunt Mildred that we associate with psychic mediums, deep-trance mediums are able to withdraw sufficiently to let the dead use their vocal cords to speak. Developing mediumistic ability to this degree requires long sessions of silent darkness, so deep-trance mediums have been rare since the advent of the radio; but as late as the 1930s there were people still working who had been able to spend the time necessary to cultivate this skill. Some of what they produced is wonderful. As with psychic mediums, I come to these accounts with a high degree of skepticism. But there have been cases where deep-trance mediums appeared to be in contact with dead folks who gave detailed and incontrovertible validation of their identities. There have been cases, too, where teams of dead people thought up clever proofs of their existence and delivered these proofs to living researchers with the help of deep-trance mediums. The testimony of the best evidence received this way is such that if mainstream science had not a century ago already been dogmatically atheistic, the fact that you will survive your death would long ago have become common knowledge.
- **Accounts Received Through Automatic Writing.** Sometimes a medium can invite a dead person to write using the medium's hands. I have read a few accounts that were purportedly written this way, and have found them to be so consistent with all the information that I have assembled from other sources that I consider them to be likely genuine.
- **Accounts by Out-of-Body Travelers.** There is a lot of evidence that we travel out of our bodies during sleep, but to learn to do it while awake is difficult. There are some, though, who seem able to do it, and the published accounts by out-of-body

travelers are generally consistent with the rest of the evidence.

- **Instrumental Transcommunication (ITC) Including Electronic Voice Phenomena (EVP).** Communicating with the dead by means of computers, tape recorders, telephones, and televisions is a very promising area that has yet to bear much fruit, in part because squabbling among living research-ers has caused their dead collaborators to withdraw.

- **Hypnotic Regression.** Some therapists help their patients regress to what appear to be past lives, and thereby help them to resolve some psychological ailments. Inevitably, it has occurred to a few to regress their patients to periods between lives. In doing so, they have uncovered some fascinating – and consistent – information.

- **Past-Life Memories of Children.** Some toddlers appear to have memories of recent past lives that ended violently. These cases seem to me to be less evidence for general reincarnation than they are evidence of what might perhaps go wrong in the process of transition.

- **Ghosts and Spirit Possession.** Ghost stories are as old as humanity, as is the idea that living people can be possessed by spirits of the dead. Can the dead appear as ghosts? Can posses-sion happen? Modern researchers have some fascinating answers.

- **Quantum Physics and Consciousness Research.** Here I am so far beyond my depth that I need a maximum-length snorkel, but fortunately there are physicists and other researchers who have done the work for us. I taught myself a little quantum physics because the picture that I had built of what appeared to be a greater reality was so consistent and sensible that I thought there had to be scientific support for it. My brief study suggests that indeed there is.

The after-death realms are surprisingly culturally dependent, and since all the death-related evidence that is readily available in English has British or North American sources, you can assume that what is said in this book will be most relevant to Americans and Britons. Evidence tells us, however, that each earth culture has its own similar after-death reality. The same sort of easy and happy survival of death is our universal birthright.

Using the Evidence

When I first began to do afterlife research, I assumed that much of what I read would be the product of wishful fantasies or the urge to make a buck. I guessed that at least half of published afterlife accounts would turn out to be inconsistent nonsense, and I thought that I could live with that. If a few of these accounts were consistent with other accounts from sources widely separated in time and place, then perhaps I could use those precious few bits to construct a picture of our after-death reality. What astounds me now is that after having read many hundreds of books, some as much as a century old, I have found that fewer than one percent of published afterlife accounts seem to be inconsistent with the glorious picture being painted by all the rest. I find it equally amazing that I cannot recall reading any duplicate death-related stories, and I have noticed no copying whatsoever. The experience has been like reading hundreds of accounts by a century's worth of travelers to Fiji. They had widely differing experiences, true, but clearly they were all describing the same complex and fascinating place.

This book is based on all those accounts, detailed in a

century's worth of books, to paint for you the glorious and downright thrilling experience that dying can be. You will live your life more productively once you understand that it will never end. And even though some of this information is by now well documented and widely known, you will be surprised to see how much more evidence there is for your own eternal life.

So I ask you to drop your pro-materiality bias temporarily. Please drop your pro-religion bias, too: if you are a Christian, you know that Jesus wants you to seek and he is glad when you find. Let's work together to look at the evidence with thoughtfulness and an open mind. This is a big topic, but it is not so big that we cannot understand it. And understanding turns out to be important.

Our Need to Know the Truth

The mortality rate is one hundred percent. As you read these words, people of every age are breathing their last in hospitals and huts, and many of them are dying in terrible ignorance and fear. Those who love them are ignorant and fearful, too, since from this side death looks like the permanent ending of a human life.

But afterlife evidence lets us study death from the opposite direction, and what we learn is that for most of us, death is an easy and enjoyable transition. It doesn't hurt and it is not frightening. After death, most of us find ourselves in a beautiful, solid, earth-like place, young and healthy in the arms of family and friends and surrounded by love. Death is the best time of your life! Wouldn't it be good if more people knew that?

It would be good, too, if more people knew that death is not fun for everyone. As you will see, the way we live our lives turns out to be extremely important, and the guidelines for how we should be living are as simple as they are absolute. Shouldn't people know that now, while they still can influence the happiness of their after-death forever?

Earth-life feels very different once you realize its purpose. Abundant afterlife evidence tells us that we are here to learn to forgive completely and learn to love others universally. That is the reason for your life. And when you see each day's annoyances as more opportunties to learn to forgive, and when you regard each creepy co-worker and each mass-murderer as another lesson in love, you see the world quite differently.

The Risk of Becoming Earthbound

There is a third reason, too, why it is important that everyone knows the truth about death. Not only does it take away fear, and not only does it teach us how to live, but each one who knows the truth about death is one less potential earthbound spirit.

It is only recently that I have come to accept the possibility that some of the dead wind up as long-term earthbound spirits. The whole idea seemed too much like ghost stories told around a campfire, and it took awhile for me to accept that this gentle afterlife process based in love might have an unfortunate glitch. But the evidence for earthbound spirits is strong, and now that I understand enough of the science of death to see how it might happen, I only wonder how common it is, and how many problems that we think are mental illness might be caused by earthbounds. This might be a terrible problem, or it might not be much of a problem. But if it happens to you, becoming earthbound is a tragedy that could linger for centuries.

Using the Evidence Selectively

One reason why so few have tried to write about the experience of dying is that to do it thoroughly you first must investigate a great many fields and accumulate a lot of knowledge, much of which relates slightly to death but is not directly on point. Think of the process as similar to figuring out how to build a house. You cut down trees and make planks and start to fit them together, only to realize that before you do anything you first must learn about engineering to keep the house from falling down, and also metalworking to make nails, cement and brickworking, and – yes! – even plumbing and wiring. So you dutifully study all these topics. Then when at last the house is standing, you slap your head as you realize that still you have to learn about paint and wallpaper, bathroom fixtures, electric lights, and glass for windows before you can build and step inside a house that is real enough to let you study the front door.

This book is about just the death experience. Therefore, in writing it I have had to put aside most of the things that I have learned in doing this research. These are some of the topics that we will not be discussing here, even though afterlife-related evidence gives us fascinating information about each of them:

- Predestination and free will
- Whether and how and by whom our lives and deaths are planned beforehand
- The power of our minds to affect reality
- The relationships among our conscious, subconscious, and eternal minds
- Reincarnation
- Angelic and ascended beings

- Pixies, fairies and sprites
- Spirit guides
- Guardian angels
- Spirit possession
- After-life progress
- Human history
- Religious history
- Quantum-based sciences
- Evolution
- Intelligent design
- Life on other planets and in other dimensions
- The nature of life
- The nature of God
- How the universe began
- How the universe will end

The more afterlife-related evidence you read, the more these other topics may seize your mind, and I wish you many happy years of study. Evidence now is so much more available than it has been for most of my life that the research that took me decades is likely to take you just a few years. The answers to your questions are there, and those answers will be consistent with this brief summary of just the parts that bear upon the death experience.

Debunkers

A few credentialed scientists have turned their attention to studying death-related phenomena. Some, like Elisabeth Kübler-Ross, Raymond Moody, and Gary Schwartz, have concentrated their efforts in death-related fields and have made important contributions. Others, however, have couched themselves as defenders of pure atheistic science and have set about trying to debunk the evidence. Years ago I read debunker literature as part of my general research, but I soon realized that debunkers are not working as serious scientists.

Debunkers begin with the fundamental premises that God does not exist and there is no such thing as an extra-material reality. So they do not open-mindedly investigate afterlife phenomena, but rather they try to disable what they perceive to be the most important claims being made in an effort to debunk the whole idea of an afterlife.

Two quick examples will show you how it's done:

1. *Tunnel Vision*. Many near-death experiences include seeing what seems to be a whirling dark tunnel with a bright light at the end. So debunkers have spun volunteers in a centrifuge or otherwise severely stressed their brains, and have found that before they lose consciousness, some volunteers suffer a narrowing of their visual field and see sparks of light. Therefore, say debunkers, near-death experiences must be the product of a dying brain! Of course, these scientists never mention the fact that many near-death experiences happen when brains are demonstrably not dying. Nor do they tell us how brains in flat-line can turn out to have been so active. And surely they don't tell us why brains in distress would produce consistent visions of fields and flowers and meetings with dead relatives, including relatives the dying person did not know were dead.

2. *Out-of-Body Illusions*. In August of 2007 the British journal *Nature* summarized an experiment simulating out-of-body experiences. Subjects were rigged to view the output of a camera pointed at their backs. When experimenters then touched

them in specific ways, the subjects described a feeling of being out of their bodies. What this might have to do with decades of actual out-of-body experiments that include long-distance validations is uncertain.

Debunking cannot be a useful strategy because none of the classes of evidence on which this book is based can be debunked entirely. Oh, you may prove that one medium is a charlatan or that someone has fabricated a near-death experience. But there are by now many thousands of afterlife-related reports, each of them so consistent with the others of its type (even when collusion is impossible) that nobody with an open mind can deny that we are seeing something real. To disprove the theory that all crows are black, it is necessary to find only one white crow (as early researcher William James famously said). Today the white crows fill the sky.

A Word About Reality

I am tempted to say cheekily, "There is no reality," but that is not precisely true. It is more accurate to say that from our perspective, no reality – not this one, and not what comes after death – can be very well comprehended. We lack the experience and the frame of reference necessary to understand what we are seeing, so it is important to emphasize here that the information in this book is expressed in human terms. What happens after death may be more real than the reality that you see around you now, but what we can know of it from here is only a narrow and human-centered glimpse.

So let us look at dying now frankly and freely, without being hobbled by religious fears or by atheistic constraints. As

Sir William Barrett said in his seminal book, ***Death-Bed Visions***
(1926, pp. 5-6):

> In considering the value of evidence for supernormal phenom-
> ena the importance of the cumulative character of the evidence must
> be taken into account. It is the undesigned coincidence of witnesses
> who have had no communication with each other that constitutes
> its value taken as a whole, whilst a single case may be doubtful or
> disproved, just as a single stick may be broken but a faggot may defy
> all our attempts at breaking a bundle of sticks.
>
> On this point Archbishop Whately has some admirable
> remarks on the value of testimony. He states: "It is evident that
> when many coincide in their testimony (where no previous concert
> can have taken place), the probability resulting from this concurrence
> does not rest on the supposed veracity of each considered sepa-
> rately, but on the improbability of such an agreement taking place
> by chance. For though in such a case each of the witnesses should
> be considered as unworthy of credit, and even much more likely to
> speak falsehood than truth, still the chances would be infinite against
> their all agreeing in the same falsehood."

Our present seemingly solid reality makes it hard for many
of us to believe that an equally solid and real afterlife is possible. I
needed to figure out some of the science underlying our going from
here to there before I could trust the afterlife evidence, and the results
of my dabbling in death-related science are summarized for you in the
next four chapters. Of course, if you don't share my need for some
scientific grounding first and you want only to know about the fun of
dying, feel free to skip ahead to Chapter 6. Either way, thanks to Sir
William and so many others, let us together part the veil....

CHAPTER TWO

THIS REALITY IS NOT THE ONLY REALITY

"There is no matter as such."
Max Planck, physicist

"And things are not what they seem."
Henry Wadsworth Longfellow, poet ("A Psalm of Life")

*"If you hold to my teaching, you are really my
disciples. Then you will know the truth,
and the truth will set you free."*
Yesua (JN 8:31-32)

*M*ost of us face two stumbling-blocks in trying to make sense of afterlife evidence. We find it hard to imagine how multiple levels of solid reality could exist in the same place simultaneously; and we cannot see how our minds could survive our deaths if they are generated by our brains. This chapter and the three that follow are intended to address these issues, and to give you a framework on which to hang your understanding of afterlife realities. But they are minimal explanations couched in layman's terms and nothing more.

Evidence tells us that there are about seven inhabited levels of after-death reality which are separated from us and from each other only by differing energy levels. How is this possible? It turns out that dying is a lot like changing channels.

Imagine that you are watching the Red Sox play the Yankees on television. The game is as real as if you were at Fenway Park. Then you flip channels and experience C-Span. Or maybe it's Local News at Six. All of these realities are taking place at once and in the same place (your television set), but each in fact is an energy pattern beaming in to your television on its own frequency. Reality is a lot like that. Think of your mind as that television set, and think of death as switching channels. You go from one solid-seeming reality to another that is equally solid and real, just as easily as it happens with television. What this implies about the character of your mind, and what it suggests about the nature of reality, are questions that we will be exploring. For now, only know that it happens this easily.

Understanding the science of death requires that you comprehend the implications of two admittedly boggling facts:

- Matter and energy and time and space are not objectively real. This universe is one heck of an illusion, but something like an illusion is what it is.
- Your mind is not generated by your brain.

The science in the chapters that follow is so vastly oversimplified that I hesitate to call it science. It is what you get when a curious non-scientist reads many popular-science materials to better understand what death-related evidence suggests about the nature of reality. The science given here is based in afterlife truths and not in our present reality, which gives us a fresh and useful perspective.

All the afterlife levels are as real as this material universe, and they exist in about the same place, so one day inevitably mainstream scientists will discover them. As they study them, they will fill in gaps and express the science of the afterlife in more traditional scientific terms. I am confident, though, that they will only confirm and not disprove what we are saying here....

CHAPTER THREE

MATTER, ENERGY, TIME AND SPACE ARE NOT OBJECTIVELY REAL

"… in quantum mechanics all particles of matter and energy can also be described as waves. And waves have an unusual property: An infinite number of them can exist in the same location."

Carlo Rovelli, physicist

"The distinction between past, present and future is only a stubbornly persistent illusion."

Albert Einstein, physicist

"The Spirit gives life; the flesh counts for nothing."

Yeshua (JN 6:63)

A discussion of all the frustrations that have plagued quantum physicists over the past century is far beyond the scope of this book. But to read about some of the awkward theories that have been put forth to solve their problems makes you wonder whether physicists might not be helped by studying afterlife evidence. After all, Occam's razor, a premise much beloved in science, holds that the simplest explanation is probably the best explanation. And surely the afterlife evidence for a greater reality provides the simplest explanation of all.

Quantum physics is a theory that posits that subatomic units called quanta are the building blocks of reality. Matter, energy, time and space are all composed of some variant of quanta, and material quanta appear to be both particles of matter and waves of energy. Physicists have repeatedly proven the truth of these principles, both experimentally and mathematically. Yet it seems that their need for physics to be physical, and perhaps their need to avoid finding God, have kept them from taking the next logical steps. Steeped in decades of studying death-related evidence and unafraid of finding God, I find some of the implications of quantum physics interesting. I think that you will, too.

Here are two facts derived from the quantum physics literature which help us begin to understand that matter, energy, time and space may not be objectively real:

1. ***Things don't achieve a fixed reality until they are consciously observed.*** In trying to determine whether a given subatomic unit is a particle of matter or a wave of energy, physicists devise experiments to look for one or the other (the most famous of

which is the Double-Slit Experiment). The more they have conducted these experiments, the more they have found that (a) particles of matter are actually waves of energy until they are observed, at which point they become particles of matter; although (b) if physicists are looking for a wave of energy, then the wave remains a wave. Not only do physicists' own minds determine the results of their experiments, but their minds may actually be creating matter or energy at the instant that they make their observations.

2. ***Measuring a quality of one subatomic particle instantly affects the same quality of a synchronized particle, even if the particles are widely separated.*** Albert Einstein called this phenomenon "spooky actions at a distance." Communication between once-synchronized but now widely-separated particles is instantaneous, and is not affected by that illusion of time and space between them. This suggests that at the subatomic level, time and space may not be objectively real.

The following fact also seizes my imagination, but it is probably a coincidence:

3. ***Most of the universe is invisible to us.*** Physicists' understanding of gravity and other forces suggests that as much as 96% of the universe is composed of "dark" energy and matter that is invisible to us, and for now, inexplicable. Afterlife evidence suggests that there are more or less seven inhabited levels of extra-material reality. If those other levels were detectable by us at all, perhaps this is how they would appear, as invisible energy and mass; or perhaps not. But they seem to take up space in the same illusory way that the material universe takes up space, and in more or less the same location, so it would not be surprising to find them affecting the universe in some fashion.

Applying Quantum Physics to What We Know About Death

What we can deduce from afterlife evidence allows us to venture ahead of quantum physicists and suggest that this is where the science may be heading:

- *Matter is not objectively real.* Matter is composed of atoms, and atoms are almost entirely empty space. I recall reading once that if the White House were an atomic nucleus, its closest orbiting electron could be as far away as Denver, and there would be literally nothing between them. At one time physicists believed that at least those subatomic particles were solid, but the more closely they studied them, the more physicists realized that subatomic particles are more empty space circumscribed by tinier orbiting particles which themselves are empty space. It begins to look as if the tiniest particles of all are just vortices of energy. Bruce Lipton, quantum biologist and author of *The Biology of Belief* (2005), tells us that if you could put a subatomic camera inside an atom, there would be nothing for it to photograph because matter is just whirling energy. Nothing is solid. Everything is waves. Of course, observation appears to force each wave to become whatever the observer seeks – either a particle of matter or a wave of energy – but since the tiniest particles are just energy vortices, it seems reasonable for us to conclude that matter is not real beyond the observation of it. Pause to consider what this means. Things seem solid to you only because your body is composed of energy vortices and your vortices conflict with those of your desk or your wall; otherwise, your hand could pass right through them.

- *Space is not objectively real.* Traveling from anywhere to anywhere on post-death levels is instantaneous. So afterlife evidence validates the quantum "spooky actions at a distance" phenomenon and suggests that in reality space has no size. The enormity of our universe is an illusion.

- *Time is an illusion, too.* It soon becomes clear as you study the evidence that after-death time is both flexible and subjective, but living as we do in our time-governed universe, it is hard to see how that is possible. You know for sure what you did this morning; you know that eventually day will be night. How is that not real? Yet afterlife evidence tells us that time is no more objectively real than are space and matter.

- *What we think of as energy is not the base creative energy.* It appears that what we call energy is just an aspect of illusory matter, so each can be transformed into the other but neither has objective reality.

So Then, What Is Real?

Evidence suggests that the only thing that we can think of as real and not just another part of the illusion is an energy-like potentiality that many researchers in this field call Consciousness. They don't always capitalize the term, but I will do that here so you won't confuse it with the general awareness that most of us refer to as consciousness. Even today, scientists remain uncertain about what our consciousness/awareness is and precisely how our brains make us conscious. But it seems that our consciousness is an aspect of Consciousness, and our brains don't generate our consciousness at all....

CHAPTER FOUR

YOUR MIND WILL LIVE ON AFTER YOUR BRAIN DIES

"The Field is the sole governor of the particle."
Albert Einstein, physicist

"Every interpretation of quantum mechanics involves consciousness."
Euan Squires, mathematician

(When the Apostle Peter was unable to walk on water)
"You of little faith. Why did you doubt?"
Yeshua (MT 14:31)

(healing a blind man)
"Do you believe that I am able to do this?... According to your faith will it be done to you."
Yeshua (MT 9:28-29)

*Y*our material brain is like a one-channel cell phone. It picks up instructions from your mind and uses them to move your body, and it communicates back to your mind whatever your body's senses are detecting. Perhaps it also does some processing, but of course your cell phone can do that too. Your brain no more generates who you are than your cell phone generates your conversations, and while people living in the Middle Ages would have found this concept hard to grasp, for those of us who rely on electronics, it ought to be an easy step. Before we discuss what evidence says about where your mind actually is, let's look at some reasons why it is so easy to be sure that your brain is just a receiver and transmitter.

Understanding the Limitations of Our Brains

For something so essential to our image of ourselves, the matter in our skulls is poorly understood. This is partly because the brain is so precious and so fragile that studying it is difficult. It is also partly because researchers expect the brain to be a lot more complex than it is, and they continue to look for aspects of it that are not there. Here are three facts:

1. ***The human genome does not code for the human mind.***
   When researchers began the Human Genome Project, many of them anticipated that the human genome would contain at least 100,000 genes. After all, *C. elegans*, a worm of fewer than 1000 cells, has about 21,000 genes in its genome. Surely humans, with our much bigger bodies and all our mental and psychological complexity, would be found to have a much bigger genome. But when early results of the Human Genome

Project were announced in 2003, it was revealed that the human genome contains fewer than 24,500 genes, which is little more than the genome of an almost microscopic worm that has little or no brainpower at all. The implications of this fact have not been well publicized, but many researchers are stunned by it. Either much of what they thought about genetics is wrong, or the brain does not generate the mind.

2. *Our brains are demonstrably inadequate as more than receivers and transmitters.* Try as they may, researchers have not been able to understand how the brain creates consciousness. Nor can they make sense of where and how our memories are stored. There are estimates that if our brains were our memory storage centers, we would have enough capacity to remember about one evening's worth of television. It has been calculated that our minds can process only 40 impressions per second at the conscious level, but 40 million impressions per second at the subconscious level, and so far scientists cannot begin to understand how our subconscious minds work. Consider the fact that people can learn to function well after a hemispherectomy, which involves the removal of half their brains. Consider also the fact that some successful adults have been found with undiagnosed hydrocephaly, a condition in which fluid occupies most of the skull and their brains are just a shell of gray matter. Your brain can no more generate who you are than your cell phone can generate a well-loved voice. As receivers and transmitters of information, though, both work well.

3. *Our brains begin to prepare to move our bodies before we are aware of the urge to move.* We are so used to the notion that our brains generate our thoughts that it comes as a surprise to learn that muscular and nervous preparations to move a digit

begin about 350 milliseconds before we decide to move it. Indeed, much of what we do in the course of living happens without prior conscious thought. We find that we have opened the refrigerator, buttoned our jacket, turned the wheel or stepped on the brake, all while thinking of other things and without any sort of deliberate intention. Some believe this means that we have no free will, but it is more likely that our nonmaterial minds make these decisions and send them to our material brains, which begin to act and only then make us consciously aware of our intention to move.

Not only are our brains inadequate as anything more than receivers and transmitters, but our primary sensory organs are surprisingly poor sources of information. Studies suggest that less than half of what we think we are seeing is based on information that comes through our eyes. Take the astonishing fact that what is projected on our retinas is upside-down, and we learn as infants to turn it right-side-up. Take the further fact that there is a blind spot in our field of vision (caused by the placement of the optic nerve) which we fill in automatically. Our hearing comes improbably through a miniscule tunnel of bones and hairs, and nerve cells pick up only a few of the sounds that are available to other creatures: animals like whales, elephants, dogs and hummingbirds can hear sounds far outside our range. And of course your touch receptors tell you that your tabletop is solid and smooth, when at the atomic level, it is neither. The fact that we so completely trust our very limited bodily senses is one reason why so many after-death levels can exist right where we are without our being much aware of them.

Our Minds Are Powerful Parts of an
Energy-Like Consciousness Matrix

I want to make it clear before we continue that I am not sure what the matrix made up (in whole or in part) of our minds really is. Some consider it to be the zero-point field, a background energy of infinite power that permeates the universe. But it may be only an aspect of the zero-point field, or it may be something else altogether. I will call it the Field for convenience, and if you must envision it as something, think of the Field as a cell-phone tower with as many unique transponders on it as there ever have been conscious beings in the universe. All our consciousnesses exist there together, and each communicates with its respective body. Your mind believes that you are in your body only because it can move that body and it picks up the sensory signals generated there.

Here are a few observations which can help us better appreciate the Field:

- *Now all manner of psychic phenomena can be more easily explained.* As we saw in the previous chapter, there is no objective time or space, and evidence tells us that the minds of every living human being and of everyone who ever has lived are part of one continuous grid. All of this makes long-suspected psychic powers like telepathy, remote viewing, and communicating with the dead probably easy to achieve. It appears that all that limits us is our belief that such things are impossible.
- *All living things may be part of the Field.* There is plentiful evidence that animals are sufficiently conscious to be part of the Field, and it appears that even plants and microbes also possess some level of consciousness. Consider an experiment first conducted by Cleve Backster in 1966 and repeated success-

37

fully many times thereafter. Backster attached a polygraph machine to the leaf of a Dracaena cane. He found that the plant registered a reaction when brine shrimp were plunged into boiling water. So far, so good. Then he discussed with a colleague what his next experimental steps might be, including perhaps burning the leaf itself, and he found that the leaf reacted violently at the instant when he thought of harming it. He later showed that even the shredded remnants of a living leaf would react to a researcher's thought of harming them. It appears from evidence that every living thing – and perhaps even every living cell – possesses some level of consciousness.

- *Longstanding medical puzzles like homeopathic medicine and the placebo effect may begin to make sense.* Researchers have long been confused by the fact that inert sugar pills can be effective medicines. According to a 1985 estimate, more than a third of medicines being prescribed at that time were placebos; and they often worked, although no one knows why. Homeopathic medicines have been used for centuries, and in defiance of cutting-edge medicine they seem to be as popular as ever. To vastly oversimplify the process, homeopathy involves succussing (banging and shaking) in water minute quantities of substances known to create whatever symptoms of disease the patient is suffering. The dilution is so great that it is likely that not a single molecule of the original substance remains in the resulting medicine, yet it often works. In both placebos and homeopathic medicine, it is almost certainly energy – generated by your mind in one case; concentrated in water by the original substance in the other – that produces whatever healing may result. Bruce Lipton says that energy is a hundred times more effective at affecting living cells than a chemical would be, so from the viewpoint of quantum medicine, these weird effects may make sense.

- ***Our minds are unimaginably powerful.*** Something that puzzled me as I did my early research was the fact that even the most advanced beings ever encountered by researchers on the most remote extra-material levels have been recognizably human. For a long time this made me suspicious. I thought it meant that people were making things up. But communications from upper-level beings suggest that human consciousness is the most advanced consciousness there is, and indeed it is a subset of the creative force from which reality springs. The implications of this are astounding, and one of the most remarkable is the fact that human minds seem to have tremendous creative power. Recall the Double-Slit Experiment, in which researchers can make either matter or energy simply by wanting one or the other. Then apply the possibility of having that kind of power to your entire life. Indeed, this may be what Yeshua means by "faith." He says, "I tell you the truth, if anyone says to this mountain, 'Go, throw yourself into the sea,' and does not doubt in his heart but believes that what he says will happen, it will be done for him. Therefore I tell you, whatever you ask for in prayer, believe that you have received it, and it will be yours." (MK: 11:23-24)

- ***Reality is fundamentally emotional.*** More and more we are learning that, far from being numbers-dry and lab-cold, reality is governed by what we might term emotion-based energy. Gregg Braden, author of ***The Divine Matrix*** (2007), said in a conference call in March of 2008 that the Field is a "soft, malleable essence of possibility" which responds to the template of what we feel and not just what we think, so "the world is a three-dimensional quantum mirror that shows us what is in our hearts... There is a growing body of evidence that what we call feeling may be the most powerful creative force known to us." As you read this, perhaps you are skeptical. But ask yourself these questions: How many successful pessimists do you know? And how many optimists seem to have events repeatedly break just right for them?

• ***Retro-intention may work as well as present intention.*** We have all heard about studies in which patients who received prayers healed sooner. There are so many such stories, and they creep so near to perhaps finding God, that this is an area where debunkers long have been active. But for every such report that they debunk, there must be a hundred more. Apparently prayer works. Now consider an experiment conducted by Leonard Liebovici. To test the power of intercessory prayer, he chose 3,393 patients hospitalized with bloodstream infections in a major medical center and conducted a rigorous double-blind study in which those prayed for were chosen at random. Neither they nor their doctors could have known which of the patients were being prayed for... because the prayers were said in the year 2000, but the hospitalizations had occurred as much as a decade earlier, in 1990 through 1994. Yet when the patients' files later were examined, it was found that patients who had been prayed for even long after they had recovered showed a significantly reduced length of hospital stay and a reduced severity of illness. This is one of many situations where we find unexpect-edly that time may not be real. We have not even begun to explore our capacity for affecting with our minds not only events in the present and future, but even – amazingly! – events long past.

A thorough investigation of the power of our minds is far beyond the scope of this book, and clearly there must be many factors at work. Studies done by Lynn McTaggart (author of ***The Field*** [2001]) and others suggest that conviction amounting to certainty improves our rate of success at manipulating events, and the best effects are achieved when many minds focus on one intention. Even despite its apparent limitations, your mind has powers far beyond any that you might heretofore have guessed, so learning to better control and use your mind is an exercise worth the effort.

There is so much evidence for the facts that matter, energy, time and space are not objectively real and that our minds are not generated by our brains that I could write a hundred more pages. I hope this taste will be enough to open your mind so you can ponder what evidence tells us actually underlies reality....

CHAPTER FIVE

CONSCIOUSNESS IS ALL THAT EXISTS

"What is it that breathes fire into the equations and makes a universe for them to describe?... Why does the universe go to all the bother of existing?"
Stephen Hawking, physicist

"The universe begins to look more like a great thought than a great machine."
Sir James Jeans, physicist

"All matter originates and exists only by virtue of a force... We must assume behind this force the existence of a conscious and intelligent mind. This mind is the matrix of all matter."
Max Planck, physicist

"The kingdom of God does not come visibly, nor will people say, 'Here it is,' or 'There it is,' because the kingdom of God is within you."
Yeshua (LK 17:20-21)

*E*verything that we think of as real is composed of Consciousness, set in place by Consciousness, and governed by Consciousness. There is nothing else. This conclusion did not originate with me, nor do I know if it can be proven mathematically; but when you study enough afterlife evidence, eventually it becomes inescapable. Religious people will find this an idea that is both familiar and comforting, but those who root for the scientific team are likely to think that I have rigged the game. To help readers for whom the notion of an underlying creative force is new or troubling, let's look first at some of the evidence.

Beginning to Make a Case for Consciousness

Knowing that Consciousness is the base creative force is likely to make your dying more fun, but it is not essential that you accept this conclusion. What happens at death remains true no matter what the larger truths may be. Still, I think that a Consciousness theory of everything is going to be inescapable. Here are three quick reasons why:

1. *What we think of as matter, energy, time and space are not objectively real.* If you want to better understand quantum physics from a layman's perspective, read Bruce Rosenblum's and Fred Kuttner's *Quantum Enigma* (2006).
2. *Our minds continuously influence reality, they are not generated by our brains, and they are all part of one Consciousness.* If you want to explore further the nature of your mind, read three of my favorites: R. Craig Hogan's *Your Eternal Self* (2008), Gregg Braden's *The Divine Matrix*

(2007), and Lynn McTaggart's *The Field* (2001).

3. *The universe is something like a conscious thought.* There is a widely accepted theory that the universe began in a physical Big Bang from a speck the size of a pencil-dot. Physicists make the amazing assumption that this enormous universe filled with billions of solid galaxies and stars began as a speck of energy and matter, even though that seems to make no sense. When we assume instead that the Big Bang was mental rather than physical, so what we see at the birth of the universe is something like the start of a conscious thought, then we can at least envision the sense of it.

We are calling the base force Consciousness because that is what many researchers call it. Frankly, I don't know what it is. It seems to be an energy-like potentiality without size or form, alive in the sense that your mind is alive, emotional and therefore likely self-aware. I haven't called it God because I don't want to tie it to your personal image of God, but I have long thought that finding the role of Consciousness explains why humankind is so innately spiritual. Don't call this force God if the name fills your head with a bearded Jehovah on his throne, smiting folks with thunderbolts for breaking a commandment or two. But if your image of God is love beyond our ability to comprehend it, then Eureka! Perhaps Consciousness is God after all.

Exploring the Amazing Implications

This is a little digression from our pursuit of the truth about death, but to help you become more comfortable with what it means for Consciousness to be all there is, I will tell you a few things that I have learned are true:

- *Although Consciousness seems to be a kind of energy, it is not like a material energy and it does not obey material laws.* What we think of as the laws of physics function only in this material universe, and this universe is just a small part of a much greater whole.

- *Each of us is a part of Consciousness, and more powerful than we can imagine.* The "I" that is in your mind is eternal: you never began and you will never end. Indeed, the very notions of "eternity" and of "beginning" and "ending" are, like "size," human ideas or constructs. Without objective time, they mean nothing.

- *There is no such thing as a private thought, since your consciousness is open to all Consciousness.* Privacy is a human illusion.

- *Matter is composed of Consciousness, so in some way, everything may be somewhat conscious.* Your dog and cat surely, but also perhaps the trees in your yard and even the rocks that ring your garden.

- *Your "I" and my "I" are not separate.* The concepts of "separate" and "the same" are human notions. It doesn't seem possible in human terms to express precisely how we are connected, but it is not wrong to say that we all are part of one great whole. When Yeshua says "Love your neighbor as yourself" (MT 22:39), we think he must mean "Love your neighbor *as if he were* yourself." But Yeshua may be telling us that you and your neighbor are part of one being.

Do you find it hard to get your mind around the notion that Consciousness is all there is? Try closing your eyes and picturing a miles-wide, miles-deep grassy plain with hazy purple mountains beyond it. Now mount the white horse standing beside you and gallop full-speed across that plain. Feel your hair blow and wind sting your eyes; feel the mane on your hands and hear hooves thudding and the whoosh of legs through grass. Now open your eyes and answer this: Where is all that happening? Where are all those miles of space, the horse, the mountains, and the sky? That's right. They are all in your mind. And the room around you is in your mind, too, and the trees outside, and the wide blue sky. Having been conditioned from infancy to see these things as real, you see them as real. You and I have learned to believe in what apparently is a collective illusion.

In a reality governed by the kind of physics that we have summarized in these four chapters, what all the evidence says about death is simple and consistent common sense. Let's look now at the fun of dying....

CHAPTER SIX

THE DEATH EXPERIENCE

"I've told my children that when I die, to release balloons in the sky to celebrate that I graduated. For me, death is a graduation."
Elisabeth Kübler-Ross, physician

"In my father's house are many rooms; if it were not so, I would have told you. I am going there to prepare a place for you. And if I go and prepare a place for you, I will come back and take you to be with me that you also may be where I am."
Yeshua (JN 14:2-3)

*O*ne of my favorite researchers in this field is Elisabeth Kübler-Ross, a physician and groundbreaking thanatologist (someone who made a career of studying death). In 1969 she published *On Death and Dying*, in which she first identified the stages through which most terminally ill people pass: denial, anger, bargaining, depression, and acceptance. Others have confirmed her observations. She was an important pioneer, but what I love most about Kübler-Ross is the tale of her personal journey. She entered the field convinced that death ends life. Then she began to hear about near-death experiences from her patients, long before Raymond Moody's *Life After Life* (1975). So toward the end of her life, Kübler-Ross began a fearless and open-minded study of what really happens when we die. She traveled out of her body with Bob Monroe; she arranged to meet her spirit guides in the flesh. By the time she entered her final illness, Kübler-Ross had become convinced that our minds easily survive our deaths.

As Kübler-Ross studied the stages of terminal illness leading to death, and as she became certain that death is not the ending, let us look now at what happens during and soon after death. And let's look at death not from this side, but from the better perspective of life over there.

Impending Death

Our bodies resist dying. They have to be rendered unusable before most of us are able to die, and this is one part of the death process which cannot be considered fun. A serious accident or a heart attack or stroke might do the job for us neatly, but most bodies lose the fight to live slowly, and the minds driving them suffer through the process. People near death can be comatose, but shortly before death – an hour or two, a day – they often wake up to enjoy what seems to be a new burst of healthy vigor as they talk with those around them, calm and pain-free. Doctors have learned to see this as a sign that death is imminent.

Deathbed Visitors

People in this pre-death stage often see people who don't seem to be there. Those around them may think they are hallucinating, but in fact the dying are being visited by predeceased loved ones. The visitors might be friends and relatives or white-robed angels or even friendly strangers. And they can be animals. One hermit who trusted no one else reportedly was met by his long-dead horse.

The dying may chat with these visitors who are invisible to the living, or they may lie staring at an empty corner because their visitors often appear in the upper corners of the room. There are rare occasions when psychic relatives sitting at a deathbed share in deathbed visions, but what is more common is for people near death to lie quietly and gaze at the corners of the room as they converse with visitors in their minds.

Occasionally dying people will have an actual glimpse of paradise. It will seem to them that one of the walls of the room has disappeared, and beyond the room they see fields of flowers, snow-topped mountains, a lake, and even buildings. All that they see is intensely colored and it is dazzlingly, heart-stoppingly beautiful: the sky is a deep and cloudless blue; the flowers are in colors not seen on earth. There are reports of panoramic deathbed visions that lasted for days while the dying person described what he was seeing. A century ago such reports were not unusual, but sadly most of the terminally ill are so heavily sedated today that if they see anything of where they are going, it is just a glimpse through a wall in the minutes before they die.

Deathbed visions are always of dead people. There are recorded cases of dying people expressing surprise at seeing a vision of someone they had believed was still alive; but every visitor is someone who has predeceased them, if only by minutes. Kübler-Ross often sat at the deathbeds of children whose families had been in auto crashes, and she (but not the child) would know who had died at the scene and who was alive in the hospital. The child would stare, and the doctor would gently ask if the child could describe what he was seeing. The child would whisper something like, "It's okay. Mummy and Peter are here for me." Kübler-Ross knew that the mother was dead, but she thought that the brother was still alive. Inevitably, though, she would later find that every family member who came to meet a child was someone who had already died. She said that the children's record was perfect. In her entire career, Kübler-Ross never sat with a child who claimed to see a vision of someone who was still alive.

We should note that people who die accidentally may not see any greeters at all until after they have left their bodies. At that point, their unplanned deaths may mean that a rescue is necessary, so they may not see someone they know but instead they might see (or just feel the presence of) one or more very advanced beings. Although it can happen, it is rare for a newly-dead person to be entirely alone.

Pre-death and at-death visions have been recognized for centuries as a common deathbed event. But why is it necessary that you see your mother or your cat or an angel at your death?

Apparently the process of dying may confuse you, especially if your survival is unexpected, so loving helpers are there to reassure and guide you. You might feel the presence of just one person, or you might see a jostling crowd. No matter the number of visitors, everyone will be someone you trust because once you are free of your body they will need to keep your close attention and persuade you to follow them away.

The Death Event

Whatever your cause of death may be, the actual moment of death is easy. All pain is gone. In fact, we are told that when death is going to be the result, any pain that a body seems to suffer is not felt by the mind at all. As death begins, you will find yourself slipping out of your body (usually from the top of the head, but occasionally from the chest) to stand beside it or hover above it. Your new body will feel normal to you, but feather-light and less substantial. You may be naked at first, but once you notice your nakedness your mind will generate clothing. Briefly you will remain connected to your former body by a glowing cord – what is commonly called a silver cord – but soon the cord will disintegrate, breaking your connection to that body.

When you are first out of your body, before the silver cord is broken, you may be able to negotiate your return. It seems generally that if your former body still is able to support life, you may be able to reclaim it if your reasons for wanting to do so revolve around your concern for loved ones who need you. Commonly mothers of young children go back, as do people who have been knocked out of their bodies accidentally and have more to accomplish in life. You are unlikely to want to go back, though, no matter how tempting that prospect seems now. You have survived, and now dead loved ones are mobbing you and hugging you and urging you to come away with them.

How It Feels to Die

Imagine moving from the pains and weakness of a decrepit body to the vigor of a healthy one so light that you can float in the air. Death feels wonderful! Indeed, by some accounts the death event includes a surge of joyous well-being that makes it feel immensely pleasurable.

Briefly, though, this is a time of danger. Nothing in your life has prepared you for this moment of being freed from the heavy shell of your material body. You feel healthy and vigorous, upbeat and powerful, and in reality you are all of that, but you are also as inept as a baby. Imagine a hundred-foot toddler blundering through a city and you will get some sense of the chaos that you can wreak on your life if things don't go right.

At first there is some confusion. You weren't really sure you would survive your death; you never imagined it would be so much fun. If you had been ill and weak, now abruptly you are strong and well. Any missing limbs have been replaced, and if you were paralyzed you now can move easily. Your senses are especially acute, and if you were deaf or blind in life, happily now you can hear and see. (A little tip from those who have been there: if something in your post-death body seems not to be working for you, simply think of it as working and it will work fine.)

So there you are, feeling wonderful, while those you left behind gasp and wail and check your former body for a pulse. Fortunately, as inept as you are, immediate guidance is available to you. Your dead loved ones are there to reassure you and urge you to follow them away.

Following your rescuers is important. Your reality now differs from your former reality in important ways that you do not yet understand, so unless you leave the death scene quickly, you are at genuine risk of getting stuck. Far from the heaven-hell-and-judgment horrors that we used to associate with death, evidence indicates that death is a natural process which frees a powerful entity from what had been a fleshly prison, and that freed entity – you, in fact – has the power to decide whether to stay or go. If you had the time to think about it, you might consider sticking around. Or if you let yourself feel your family's pain – in your new condition you can feel it easily – maybe you would be unable to leave them. But sticking around after your body has died never is a good idea. Before you have the chance to consider your options, your dead mother or a loving angel will hustle you right out of there.

Interestingly, if you look back at your death-scene as you leave it, you will find that the room and your relatives are becoming shimmery and insubstantial. The post-death levels are not like stripes, but they are more like a rainbow of colors whose margins blend into one another. So as you enter the post-death levels, your perspective shifts. Your new body and your new environment become reassuringly solid, while the formerly solid level you are leaving grows insubstantial and fades away.

Crossing the Bridge, Entering the Tunnel, Going Through the Wall, or Whatever

The notion of a tunnel that ends in a light has become a part of our folklore, so it may surprise you to know that when you die, you may not see a tunnel. Some who have died report that they seemed instead to walk across a bridge. Some stood and walked right through a wall, while others found themselves in paradise without noticing a precise transition.

After reading about hundreds of near-death experiences and completed deaths, I have a hunch – just a hunch, mind you – that most deaths involve either falling asleep before death and waking up in the afterlife, or stepping from one reality to the other under the care of an advanced being. The tunnel of our folklore may be a kind of wormhole to convey you through earthbounds and the lowest outer-darkness level. It appears that a more spiritually advanced guide can protect you from unpleasant encounters, but your mother or your uncle may be unable to keep you safe in transit without use of the tunnel. Whatever its purpose may be, whether or not you enter any tunnel that you see, and indeed whether you cross a bridge or pass through a hole in a wall, if you are awake at your moment of death the decision to leave seems to be up to you.

Entering the Afterlife

Once you have departed your death scene, and depending on your mental condition, you may enter a period of grayness, or you may go to sleep altogether. People who have experienced the grayness describe it as walking through a fog. Typically they no longer see their companions, but they know they are still there. And the grayness soon passes. If a gray period happens to you, just keep talking with those who are escorting you and travel on, knowing that soon the fog will break.

People who have been very ill, and those who die traumatically, often sleep through the death process and wake up in a hospital with loved ones and nurses caring for them. These hospitals are unlike hospitals on earth. Some are Victorian-style brick buildings with patient rooms and beautiful gardens, and some are more like pavilions that shelter many patient beds, again surrounded by gardens. And it isn't only the sick and traumatized who tend to sleep through their deaths. Even people who haven't died in what we might see as unusual distress will often go to sleep before death and then wake up with friends and family around them in a heavenly replica of a favorite earth-home.

One wonderful thing about the death experience is that it seems to be quite carefully tailored to each person's needs. Those heavenly glimpses that we have beforehand; the choice of who will lead us from the death scene; whether there is a period of sleep; and whether or not a hospital is needed: all these decisions are made for us in a spirit of unearthly love so we can have the best experience possible.

Emergency Surgery

The first post-death step for some of us is a little medical treatment. Issues that we might see as mind-damage, like brain injuries or senile dementia, seem to slough off with the physical body, so our minds at death are altogether well. No, the real post-death mind-damage seems to be wrong perceptions. Perhaps you were paralyzed or riddled with cancer, or you suffered some bodily trauma. Simply dying might not fix those illusions, so some of us will have emergency surgery.

Each account that I have read of medical treatment soon after death is touching and sweet. Whatever you expect real doctors to look like is just how your medical team looks, and whatever you expect to see in an earthly operating room is there around you. You are told that you have a problem that fortunately these doctors can fix. Your team then prepares you for surgery and works until the last stitch is in place, when you are told that you are now completely well.

Sometimes even post-death surgery is not enough to remove our illusions, so then occasionally other things are tried. One recorded tale is of a youth who was so despondent because of a genital injury received in World War I that even his post-death surgery didn't cure him. So he fell asleep, and he woke up in the arms of a beautiful young woman who proceeded to make love to him. This is one of only a few accounts of actual physical sex after death, but I include it because it is so consistent with the way the newly dead are treated. Whatever you might need to aid your healing, you have it. (If the thought of no post-death sex is a downer, you should know that apparently there is something better – a kind of pleasurable body-melding – that has no morality attached to it.)

The point of our whole transition process seems to be to remove the negative effects of our earthly life (which we soon come to see as just a bad year in school), and prepare us for the glorious reception that most of us are about to receive....

CHAPTER SEVEN

THE START OF YOUR AFTER-DEATH LIFE

"Do not judge, or you too will be judged. For in the same way you judge others, you will be judged, and with the measure you use, it will be measured to you."
Yeshua (MT 7:1-2)

"You judge by human standards;
I pass judgment on no one."
Yeshua (JN 8:15)

*B*ecause so many die traumatically or die as a result of illness, it may be that most of us wake up in hospitals or in the quiet of our post-death homes. My guess now is that fewer than half of us enter through reception gardens. But these gardens make such a good introduction to the reality that we enter at death that we are going to assume that you have remained awake through your whole death process and you haven't needed medical help. So you have arrived at a reception garden after a reasonably well-lived life.

Entrance

The reception gardens are located on the middle post-death levels, and they are enormous. Everything on the nonmaterial levels seems expansive and empty of people after our crowded earthly lives, but once we are used to moving by thought we can travel at once to anywhere we like.

The British and North American reception areas most often described are what you would expect – garden nooks with trees and benches, long park vistas, and elegant stone buildings. Birds sing and there might be music, but overall it is utterly quiet. Not only are there no motor sounds, but since you are hearing with your mind, there are no artifact sounds, no ringing in your ears, and even the smallest sound is crisp and bright. The scent of flowers is in the air, and everything is bathed in a clean white light.

New arrivals are stunned by the beauty of this place and by the plain relief of its earth-like normality, but what is most amazing is the feeling of love and peace that pervades it. Whatever nervousness you had about the afterlife, about judgment or purgatory or just about the boredom of living on a cloud forevermore, all of that quickly dissipates. You are in heaven, and you know it. You listen to birds and the splash of fountains. You study the trees and flowers all around, some of which are familiar to you, although others have never grown on earth. Wonderfully, everything seems to be alive, even the air and the pure white light and the stone-like materials that make up the buildings. But what you will find most remarkable is the seemingly conscious vegetation.

This detail is so often mentioned, and the accounts of it are so consistent, that it is one of the things about this place of which I am most certain. Flowers and trees here are permanent. Leaves never shrivel and blossoms never fade, so once a garden is in place, it stays in place until someone rearranges it. And amazingly, each individual plant appears to be loving and self-aware. Think of it! Flowers turn toward you as you pass them; trees reach branches down to caress you. The vegetation gives off a glorious scent, and it sheds an energy that is nourishing to people and produces a light, harmonic music that most folks find hard to describe. The shock of joy that all this brings is such that some new arrivals will stay awhile in their reception gardens, sitting on a bench with their greeters perhaps and enjoying the fact of their survival. A bird might perch on your finger, or perhaps a childhood pet might appear and jump into your lap to be petted.

Some accounts of reception-garden arrivals say that there were people in the distance. Most were in the long and luminous tunics that are the normal mode of dress, but a few were in period clothing since apparently there is no dress code.

Whether you have awakened in a hospital or in the quiet of a post-death home or traveled awake to a reception garden, you have now arrived. This heaven is more like earth than you imagined, but still it is so very different – it is at once both familiar and fabulous. Everything is made of loving energy, most things seem to be somewhat conscious, and because nothing ever decays and night never falls, there is a permanent, timeless beauty to it all.

Time feels very different here so it might not seem to happen for awhile, but sometime soon after you arrive, you will have some variant of two experiences: you will party hearty and you will be judged.

After-Death Geography

Evidence suggests that there are more or less seven major after-death levels separated only by their rates of vibration (the term most commonly used), with each level including a seemingly infinite number of places based in part on worldwide cultural norms. Interestingly, to die accidentally in a foreign country might result in your arrival in that region's after-death reality, and you may be stuck there until you think to call to your loved ones to come and take you home.

If you would find an after-death diagram helpful, George W. Meek's *After We Die, What Then?* (1987) contains a simple and useful one, as long as you remember that all the levels exist in about the same place. Briefly, the lowest after-death level is the outer darkness that Yeshua warns about, full of tormented people condemned to ages of misery living in foul-smelling squalor. The highest levels are for people so spiritually advanced that they live in bliss. Levels Three through Five are an earth-solid paradise, often called by the Viking term the *Summerland*, where the newly dead can recover from the effects of their earthly lives and enjoy a life of play and work and learning. And to answer an obvious question, cultural differences gradually disappear as we progress toward Level Five, so by Level Six there appears to be only one universal human reality.

Life Review and Judgment

Some people have two life reviews, a quick one before death and a formal one afterward. Our folklore is full of stories of people who saw their lives pass before their eyes when they were in immediate fear of death, and many of these appear to be genuine life reviews, in which those facing death get to feel life events from the perspectives of the people they affected. But unlike the formal review that follows death, the before-death review usually happens without guidance in interpreting what is seen and felt. Those who have had pre-death life reviews tell us the experience was over in an instant, yet still they saw every event of their lives, a notion that folks stuck in linear-time thinking may find difficult to believe. From an after-death perspective, though, time is so elastic that we know that such time-compression happens easily.

After our pre-death life review, if we have one, come death and the after-death events that end for some of us in that beautiful park. Some people go directly from there to their formal life reviews, while for others the life review is delayed until after they have begun their new existence. So your life review may not seem to happen for awhile, but since that day of judgment looms so large, let's consider it now and get it out of the way.

Like everything else about our deaths, our life review and judgment seem to be lovingly arranged to suit each of us and give us the best and most productive experience possible. For some, the life review happens in a quiet room in a childhood home with a single sympathetic guide there to help. For others, it is a formal affair less gently done before a council of elders. Some of those who arrive at the North American Summerland will have their life reviews in a classic stone building of enormous size, in a big quiet room with benches against the walls and what appears to be a giant central globe.

Accounts of life reviews usually say that there were people there to help. Some were very advanced beings, while others were guides who helped the new arrival during the lifetime just completed. Those being judged feel comforted and supported by their presence, which is good, since a life review can be a harrowing experience.

People who have been there tell us that their life reviews were less about the events themselves than they were about personally experiencing each of the other participants' feelings. For everyone that you ever bullied or cheated or started nasty rumors about, each aggrieved spouse or child, and everyone else that you ever wronged in your entire life, you will be made to feel as you made each of them feel. Fortunately, you also will feel the good effects of all your actions, and many say that in retrospect, experiencing the joys that they gave to others during their lives made their life reviews rather wonderful. I say "in retrospect," because first they had to deal with all the harm that they had done and get to the place where they could forgive themselves.

Precisely where the incidents of your life will appear seems to vary. Some people say they saw them in that big central globe, while others say the incidents somehow happened in the room around them. It may be that it can be done in various ways, depending on what our advisers think is best for us. And similarly, some of the dead review their lives from birth forward, while for many others the life review goes backward from the death event. The whole experience is quite subjective. But however it happens, each participant's emotions are felt as if we are living them in that moment.

These formal life reviews seem to take awhile, although, again, *awhile* here is subjective. We are allowed to experience our life reviews without much comment from those around us, but if we become upset, our helpers might say something like, "You were just learning then," or "It will get better." No attempt is made to tell us that the smallest harm done by us was unimportant. In fact, we are made to see that everything we did was much more important than we knew. We seem to be meant to realize that the standards for living our lives were higher than we ever imagined while on earth, but that nevertheless our task now is to forgive ourselves for each mistake.

A few of the dead have mentioned that their life reviews included a requirement that they also forgive others, but that seems to be easy from the perspective of eternal life. Perhaps from here our earthly grudges seem silly, especially given our new ability to feel and understand things from other people's perspectives. For whatever reason, few accounts even mention a need to forgive others, since most people going through a life review are so staggered by their need to forgive themselves.

Forgiving yourself is hard. People who have been through a life review have said that the worst part was not reliving their big mistakes – they were prepared for those. What was hardest was seeing how many times they had said or done some cruel thing, and how many times they had ignored a chance to do for someone else some little kindness.

There in the intimacy of your childhood bedroom or in a great stone hall with elders around you who can read your mind, all the excuses that you might think of now – the blaming of others, the self-justifications – none of them are possible. Instead, you must confront your deepest feelings, recognize every shabby thing about yourself, and still forgive yourself as you would hope for forgiveness from a loving God.

Here is one of the remarkable insights sprung from decades of doing this research: neither God nor any religious figure ever appears to be your judge. Instead, you are your own judge. On close reading (see Appendix II) the Gospel words of Yeshua seem to confirm this, but it is a detail that most Christians have missed. Oh, some accounts of life reviews include a council of elders who carry on discussions of what the living might see as minor mistakes. But even then, the point of the experience is to help us face whatever harm we did in life, and then help us to forgive ourselves completely.

If we cannot forgive ourselves right away, there is counseling and there are classes meant to help us learn and get us there. So much help is available that it seems that most of those who make it to the Summerland levels eventually manage self-forgiveness. That is a good thing, since forgiveness raises our rate of vibration while an inability to forgive lowers it. Eventually, if we cannot get past a remorseful dwelling on past mistakes, we will find ourselves drifting toward the lower levels, toward the outer darkness and away from those we love.

Reception and Partying

At some point after a successful death, there will be what we might call a reception. These events are highly subjective, so folks who are private by nature might choose to spend time with a few old friends, while others who enjoy partying are in for the party of their lives.

Most welcoming receptions happen in a location that is important to the new arrival. For some it is in their favorite earth-home, re-created here to the last detail. For others, it might be in or near a wonderful Greek-temple-style building, or even in a great public building constructed of living luminescent glass.

Touching tidbits about post-death homes are included in so many accounts that we ought to pause and mention some of them. Single people and the first spouse to die are usually taken to their childhood homes or to the homes of predeceased friends or relatives. Loving husbands will re-create their wives' favorite earth-homes down to dishes and furniture, but they sometimes alter them. One wife complained that her husband had built their beloved house well enough, but he had built its mirror image, so left and right were reversed; another said that her husband had built their house with the ugly addition she had not let him build in life. I once read a detailed account of a humble soul who had died homeless, for whom a mansion had been built that he found uncomfortable and overwhelming. And in another account, a wife had lovingly made a live-aboard yacht for her husband who had wanted one all his life. We can keep living wherever we first are taken, or we can move on, as we like. But before we move on, we will be visited by a bevy of dead loved ones.

I call this a reception or a party, but dead people seldom use these terms. For most, this is just a time when folks they used to know keep turning up. The newly dead find it most remarkable that no matter what their age at death, nearly all the people who greet them now appear to be in their prime of life; and even people with whom they had not gotten along on earth are glad to see them. They enjoy repeated reunions with hugs and back-slapping and the giddy awareness that – by gosh! – here we are together again, and isn't it all too wonderful! Sometimes food is served. Sometimes there is music, or gifts are given which might have a special meaning. Often the conversation is verbal because the newly arrived are used to talking, although after we have been here for awhile we will slip into a telepathic communication which those who are used to it say is better.

Our judgment and our reception begin our post-death life. From here we will move on to build an existence that might include some combination of taking classes, doing crafts, attending concerts, reading, playing at sports, assisting and even rescuing others on earth and on the lowest after-death level, and touring a greater reality that is larger and more varied than the one we left. Infinite learning is here for us, from classes in music and art and earth history to classes in advanced love and forgiveness, and even classes in mind-creating that I find both wonderful and hard to believe. There is a lot more to do here than there was in the life we left, and – as my Depression-bruised mother-in-law told me – wonderfully, "You don't need money."

What About the Children?

Dead children grow up here in a few earth-years in an atmosphere of such absolute love that some who didn't die as children report being a bit envious of them. Children who have familiar dead relatives might be raised by a grandma or an aunt in her home, but most children are met by what appear to be angels and reared in special homes and villages set a little apart from the adult areas. There is evidence that even miscarried and aborted fetuses will grow up here and later help greet their parents. Nurturing these children is special work, much-coveted and devotedly done. Parents who have lost a child should know their child is safe and happy and will be waiting to welcome them as a young adult they will be thrilled to love.

Death Is Meant to be Wonderful

The more we study death-related evidence, the more apparent it becomes that we are meant to enjoy our deaths and the greater life that follows them. The fun of it all is not inadvertent. Instead, the fun seems to be designed individually for each of us as an infinitely powerful Parent would lovingly plan adventures for each child, and it seems to be only our own pre-death willfulness that can keep us from enjoying the experience. We will talk in Chapter 9 about some of the ways in which we might screw up our deaths, but first let's explore a few post-death details....

CHAPTER EIGHT

SOME ENJOYABLE DETAILS

"Therefore I tell you, do not worry about your life, what you will eat; or about your body, what you will wear. Life is more than food, and the body more than clothes…. Who of you by worrying can add a single hour to his life? Since you cannot do this very little thing, why do you worry about the rest?"
Yeshua (LK 12:22-26)

"But love your enemies, do good to them, and lend to them without expecting to get anything back. Then your reward will be great, and you will be sons of the Most High, because he is kind to the ungrateful and wicked. Be merciful, just as your Father is merciful."
Yeshua (LK 6:35-36)

"Heaven and earth will pass away, but my words will never pass away."
Yeshua (MK 13:31)

*S*ome things about the period soon after death are reported so frequently that I am confident they are true. They amuse and often delight me, so perhaps they will do the same for you.

I want to stress again that nothing said in this book is my own speculation. Except where noted otherwise, everything said here is mentioned more than once in the afterlife literature, and most of these details can be found repeatedly. I know that some of what I am telling you seems far beyond too good to be true. I also found it unbelievable at first, which was why I kept doing research even after I realized that the afterlife details are consistent across communication styles and through a century of documentation. Unbelievable findings require repeated confirmation! If you are straining to believe, then I urge you to do some of your own research. The more of it you do, the more clearly you will see that an afterlife that seems too good to be true is wonderfully true nonetheless.

Don't forget that a lot of the afterlife evidence is as much as a century old, and those communicating with us then would have died before 1920. Their Summerland won't be our Summerland! There are Flappers and Bobby-Soxers and Beats there by now, and the oldest Baby Boomers will soon be flooding in. I smile to think how the Summerland is changing as the Greatest Generation builds its bungalows and jazz and rock & roll compete with classical music. Don't worry that the Summerland as described here seems to be a tad exotic, since by the time that you and I get there it is going to feel like home.

Now for a few fun facts to give you a foretaste of your Summerland life:

- To answer a common question first, some people do attend

their own funerals. Not everyone does it, and many attendees will have helpers there to comfort them and draw them away if necessary. But when the ties of love are strong and a death has been relatively easy, there is evidence that many of us enjoy this last earth-party of our lives.

- Few dead people care about their former bodies. Some express frustration that their loved ones are wasting energy and emotion in visiting and tending what they consider to be empty graves.

- Dying does not in itself bring enlightenment. This often surprises the recently dead, who express frustration at finding themselves exactly the same people that they were before they died.

- We live on the middle post-death levels in a constant pure white light that is brighter and more diffuse than sunlight, although it doesn't affect our eyes in the way that sunlight would.

- There is no sun, there are no stars, there is no night, and it never snows or rains, but if you want to enjoy a sunset or night or snow or rain you can have them. Temperatures remain in the mid-seventies, but cold-weather sports are available. Indeed, some accounts suggest that the Scandinavian Summerland includes snow.

- Breathing here fills our bodies with a living and energizing air which is all the nourishment we need.

- Although we don't need to eat or drink, if we want to eat or drink we can have what we like and enjoy feasting for as long as we like. We lack digestive organs, so our illusory food and drink disappears. Apparently nearly everyone soon decides that food and drink are too much bother.

- After the post-death nap that most people take, we never need to sleep again. Our lives in the Summerland are repeated periods of activity followed by periods of doing quieter things in constant daylight. Our bodies and minds never tire.

- We can appear at whatever age we prefer. Most people choose to be the person they were in their prime of life, but that is up to them. Some like age fifty better, so they have a few wrinkles and gray in their hair. Some even choose to take on the appearance of what they believe is a prior earth-lifetime. There is evidence that we can learn to change our appearances to suit ourselves, so someone might first appear to you as an old codger you knew in life, and then seem to grow progressively younger. For those newly arrived, their progression or regression in age after death can be gradual, as can be the loss of earth-disabilities as we realize those infirmities are gone.

- We can dress as we like. For some it feels important to retain the clothing that they wore in life, so you can see people in 19th-century garb and maybe in 1920s dress and in almost anything else. Most people eventually stop caring how they dress, and they revert to the floor-length, long-sleeved tunics that we associate with angels. Most tunics are in pastel colors, and their luminescent fabric softly glows. There are suggestions that the color and details of the tunic and its belt (and also of other clothing, like the occasional cape or hat) are reflective of our spiritual status.

- The after-death levels are a spiritual hierarchy in which we all are working to advance, but without objective time there is no sense of hurry to our progress.

- Here our earth-status counts for nothing. When Yeshua said, "Many who are first will be last, and the last first" (MK 10:31), he meant it.

- Most after-death communication is telepathic. Somehow this does away with the problem of different earth-languages, so once we are accustomed to telepathy, we can converse with anyone we like.

- We can read the minds of those we left on earth, and we can communicate with them by thought, but living people seldom notice our messages. A few of the dead are able to manifest on earth physically under certain conditions, and some can affect electricity, but most of us are unable to do more than produce a whiff of some distinctive scent. Real communication with the living is hard and it requires a lot of training and practice, but that is not the only reason why those on earth so seldom hear from dead loved ones. From the perspective of eternity, earth-lives are brief, and we can check in whenever we like to be sure that those we left are doing fine. Meanwhile, we are ever busier as our ties to earth grow dim. To put it bluntly, after our deaths, we have many more exciting things to do than to try to deliver evidence of what our loved ones will soon find out for themselves.

- Colors in the Summerland are not limited to the visible-light spectrum, so there are colors here that are impossible for the living to imagine. This comes up especially in reference to flowers, many of which are in unearthly colors.

- Flowers are everywhere in the Summerland. Each blossom is permanent and gorgeous and fragrant, and gardening is fun because it consists of setting full-grown flowering plants and forever just enjoying them, with no need to water, feed or weed them.

- Water is abundant here. It is crystalline and it sparkles like earth-water, but it is very different indeed. Many accounts say

that it seems to be alive, and it gives off the same sort of ador-
ing and enlivening energy and subtle music that come from the
vegetation. What most astonishes new arrivals about the water
is how different it feels, like touching silk, and the fact that
we can bathe in a lake fully clothed and walk out of it dry.
Descriptions of the water on the after-death levels sound a lot
like what Yeshua was describing when he said, "If you knew
the gift of God and who it is that asks you for a drink, you
would have asked him and he would have given you living
water." (JN 4:10) Some Christians have assumed this was a
reference to baptism, but I have found no evidence that being
baptized makes an afterlife difference. So it may be that his
reference to "living water" is yet more evidence that Yeshua
was personally familiar with after-death realities.

- Birds and small wild animals are mentioned in the literature,
but every larger animal in the Summerland is somebody's
beloved pet. Although animals have species-specific "group
souls" to which they return at death, those that have been loved
by people can develop an independent existence. Our relatives
care for each of our pets, or else each pet lives with others of
its kind while it waits for us to arrive. If they are especially
important to us, our pets might come as our before-death
guides. More often, they wait with our other loved ones, and
sometimes the people waiting for us find it hard to get through
all the dogs and cats overjoyed to greet the new arrival. Like
people, our pets are now young and healthy. Like people, they
neither eat nor eliminate. And it isn't only cats and dogs that
await us, but our beloved horses are here for the riding and
there are farm and circus animals. Of course, it goes without
saying that here the lion does lie down with the lamb.

- It appears from many accounts that in the Summerland we can have what we want. Any long-lamented article, any lost toy, any work of art or piece of clothing – we need only think of it, and we have it. The point may be to get us past all sense of material longing or lack; but when we first arrive, it is wonderful to simply think of something and find it there.

- Many after-death accounts include a wonderful library (which seems to contain more scrolls than books) where we can read about literally anything.

- There is a lot of evidence for reincarnation, but linear time is an illusion, so apparently our lives on earth are somehow being lived all at once. We cannot begin to understand the reincarnation process before we die, so researching how it happens and retrieving events from both our past lives and our lives to come is high on many people's lists.

- There is evidence that we can choose to experience any event in the history of the earth. We can walk with dinosaurs, attend the Continental Congress, and generally satisfy all our curiosity.

- We need to be taught how to do it, but travel in the after-death levels is mostly by thought, and it is instantaneous. We can walk if we prefer walking, but if we choose to dispense with walking we can go anywhere instantly. With thought-travel we don't need vehicles, but those who in life enjoyed cars or boats or planes can have and use them for as long as they matter.

- As we become more spiritually advanced, we can travel to any place on earth and any place in the post-death reality that is at or below our own vibrational level. With the assistance of very advanced beings, we also can journey to higher levels and taste the greater joys awaiting us there.

- Our minds are so much better without the interference of a material brain that we can learn with amazing ease. There seems to be a special demand for teachers of musical instruments and teachers of painting and various crafts. We are told that it is possible to learn to play piano with the greatest composers and learn to paint under legendary artists.

- Music here seems to be a near-obsession. Many accounts exist of vast amphitheaters very like those in ancient Greece, where it seems to each of the audience members that he or she is sitting in the middle of the first row. And we don't only hear the music better than we heard it on earth but we also see it as colorful clouds and shapes above the performers. Classical music is favored, but modern artists also perform, and three names that I have seen mentioned are Frank Sinatra, Elvis Presley and John Lennon. (I have read that Elvis has decided to stay at an accessible level and keep performing until all his fans have died and seen him in person. Not sure if that is true, but it makes a great story.)

- Besides musical performances of all descriptions, we also enjoy plays and talent acts. And it isn't only the famous who perform. There are hints that anyone who wants to write or perform can find a ready audience.

- Structures here can be built in two ways. We can construct them board-by-board, or we can enlist the help of more-advanced beings and have them mind-created. I once read an account of a farmer who was having a house built for his daughter on a heavenly replica of the family farm. Advanced beings helped him design it, and at the appointed moment, they concentrated their energies so the planned building shimmered into existence.

Never have I read an account of a post-death atheist. God is as happily taken for granted in the Summerland as life and light. All the mentions of God that I have seen say that He is at the Celestial Level, and His energy is such that for anyone to get even close to God without first maturing spiritually is impossible. They say He is the source of all the light on the after-death levels, which is why the lowest level is dark and the levels above it grow gradually brighter. He is never seen, but no one minds that since there is a general understanding that each of us is spiritually advancing and eventually we all will join Him. No throne, no beard, no vengeful anger (and of course no human gender), but instead an infinitely powerful, infinitely loving and all-pervasive energy – that is what they tell us God is. (I apologize to atheists, but I am not making this up. You might read some of the accounts by people who have made this trip during the past 150 years. And please try to be open-minded whenever your own death starts to happen, because there is probably a hollow heaven for people who are adamant atheists – we discuss hollow heavens in the next chapter – and emphatically you do not want to go there!)

Two things for which I have found no evidence are a fiery hell and an actual devil. P.M.H. Atwater, author of *Beyond the Light* (Revised Edition - 2009), says that about one in seven near-death experiences is unpleasant or hellish, but nearly all of these involve the outer darkness populated by demon-like people that we will discuss in Chapter 9. The only evidence for a fiery hell is a handful of accounts of near-death experiences in which people thought they were in fire, but as soon as they called for help they were out of that illusion. Nasty, demonic people do exist in the outer darkness and as earthbounds, and they are scary, but their power is feeble. If you stand up to them, they back away. It appears from all the reading

I have done that there really is no horned devil, just as there is no bearded god. Rather, very advanced beings suggest that we humans have created all the evil that exists. (You might point out here that not being found is just the devil's cleverest trick, and you might be right, but I don't think so.)

Oddly, there is rather little religion practiced on the after-death levels other than in the hollow heavens that we will mention in the next chapter. From the glimpses that I have seen, some dead clergymen feel compelled to correct whatever they had taught on earth, so they hold classes on these subjects. There are references here and there to Summerland worship services for people who miss those religions trappings, but very few. I am tempted to joke that having practiced religion, by now these folks have mastered it, but it may be that they feel close enough to God now not to need religion.

While the Summerland seems to hold little religious practice, science here has a prominent place. People with scientific training often join other scientists in laboratories, where they tell us they are working on earth's next scientific advances. Once they have made some discovery or invention for which they think the living are ready, they tell us that they impress it on the minds of a few living scientists. They say this is why breakthroughs sometimes happen in two or three places at once. By several accounts, Thomas Edison continues to try to find a way to establish telephone communications between earth and the Summerland. We are told he started working on it while alive and then continued this work after death.

After we die, we cannot fake anything. We are drawn to the vibrational level to which our spiritual status suits us, and while we can easily visit lower levels, it seems to be unbearable to go higher. I read an account by someone who was anxious to advance to Level Four, so a friend of his who lived there brought him up for a visit.

The visitor described his visit as unbearable, something like being unable to breathe, so he returned humbly to Level Three and worked to raise his own vibration. When he later took a class on Level Four, he was thrilled to find that while he was aware of the higher vibration, now he didn't mind it.

The middle after-death levels end at about Level Five, above which are the Causal (or Mental) Level and the Celestial Level. There are suggestions of sub-levels, and sometimes the names and details of the levels will shift a bit in various accounts; but more than a century of communicating with the dead has given us a consistent picture of seven primary after-death levels.

Residents of the Causal Level can be revered teachers on lower levels, where they often appear as elders. Advanced beings tell us that the Causal Level is composed of blissful mind-energy and little of it is material, although Causal Level visits in the literature include descriptions of wonderful palaces. Perhaps these were just visits to the top of Level Five, and not really visits to the Causal Level; or perhaps palaces can appear on the Causal Level temporarily for the benefit of visitors.

We know little about the Celestial Level. I have found no evidence that anyone who has earned entrance there (with the possible exception of Yeshua) ever has unmistakably communicated with us. There are references in the afterlife literature and in the Bible to visits to "level seven" or "the seventh heaven," but each of these accounts includes much that is humanlike. My hunch now is that these were visits to the top of the Summerland and not higher.

Just as the material universe is a grand illusion, so the reality that we enter at death must also be seen as illusory. It seems to us as we consider it from here to be more obviously mind-created, although those who live there often say that the afterlife reality is actually more real than the material universe.

Our Summerland period seems to be a time of decompression and play and learning after our difficult lives on earth. It seems meant to help us consolidate all the lessons that we have learned and to give us a gradual transition toward the upper levels where few illusions exist.

There is evidence that without the illusions, what we are is specks of light. Robert Monroe's out-of-body accounts in his *Journeys Out of the Body* (1971), *Far Journeys* (1985), and *Ultimate Journey* (1994) contain some descriptions of people as specks of light against darkness, which is how the greater reality might look when few illusions are in place. More-advanced beings seem to find this normal, but those of us used to life on earth might be shocked to find so big a change so we are protected by remaining in illusion.

We are told by upper-level beings that we cannot understand what is going on so there is no point in trying. It seems from evidence that our rough planet is a kind of kindergarten where we can learn the basics – how to forgive and how to love – and once we have mastered those skills, we will be ready to move up to primary grades. Like other kindergarteners, we are told to concentrate on our learning now, and to trust that each unimaginable lesson in all the many grades to come is going to be enjoyable and worth the effort in a system that appears to have been designed in perfect love for our ultimate good.

People who have been taught that heaven is an eternity of worshiping God may find it hard to believe that the reality that we enter at death is centered on human pleasures. But would you want your own beloved children to spend eternity groveling before you and telling you how great you are? Of course not. And apparently neither does God. As Yeshua says, "Which of you, if his son asks for bread, will give him a stone? Or if he asks for a fish, will give him a snake? If you, then, though you are evil, know how to give good gifts to your children, how much more will your Father in heaven give good gifts to those who ask Him!" (MT 7:9-11) It may be that our learning and growing spiritually toward a reunion with God is all the worship that He wants or needs.

This completes our account of the death experience for people who have lived decent lives and died without significant glitches. If you want to know more, go to Appendix I and learn more to your heart's content. For now, only know that no matter how rough this brief earth-life may seem to you, in fact you are a powerful eternal being and you are loved more than you can imagine.

Most of us can feel safe in knowing that a Summerland level is where we are heading, but for some people death is not fun. Let's consider now what might go wrong....

CHAPTER NINE

WHAT CAN GO WRONG?

"I say to you that many will come from the east and the west, and will take their places at the feast with Abraham, Isaac and Jacob in the kingdom of heaven. But the subjects of the kingdom will be thrown outside, into the darkness, where there will be weeping and gnashing of teeth."
Yeshua (MT 8:11-12)

"You have heard that it was said to the people long ago, 'Do not murder, and anyone who murders will be subject to judgment.' But I tell you that anyone who is angry with his brother will be subject to judgment. Again, anyone who says to his brother, 'Raca,' is answerable to the Sanhedrin. But anyone who says, 'You fool' will be in danger of the fire of hell."
Yeshua (MT 5:21-22)

here are people for whom death is not fun. I don't
know the percentage of those who die who then encounter
problems, but the primary cause of after-death issues seems to be
flat ignorance. If you have learned the truth and lived a reasonable
life, you should have nothing at all to fear. Still, no account of the
death experience would be complete if we did not mention some
of the things that can go wrong. Perhaps there are other ways in
which you could have an unhappy death, but these are all that I
have seen mentioned, and I believe they cover the field.

You Might Get Stuck

Apparently many newly-dead people are confused. The properties
of their bodies are different; the powers of their minds are different; their sense of time and space is different; and just their having
so easily survived what they had thought could be a terminal event
may be confusing and alarming. No one living can see or hear them
now, and unless they soon notice their rescuers or a tunnel nearby,
they may become so focused on their efforts to get the attention
of the living that they no longer see anything else. In this condition, evidence suggests that dead people can remain stuck in place
for what might be hundreds of earth-years. Many of them resume
their before-death routines in what apparently feels to them like
one continuous afternoon. Strangers come and go. They feel
ignored and hurt, but things still look to them as they looked at
their moment of death, so they have no idea that time is passing.
These are classic ghosts, and generally just having somebody

psychic help them realize that they are dead and there is a tunnel waiting will be enough to set them on their way.

You Might Be Afraid

Some people refuse to follow their rescuers, often because they are afraid of hell. They see loved ones and a tunnel or bridge nearby, but it seems safer to stay where they are. As with those who are only confused, the fearful newly dead soon lose their ability to perceive the after-death dimensions, so they are stuck outside of time in a static reality that they alone can see. For them, too, life seems to continue as a single day that might last for centuries. This seems pleasant enough, but it is tragic when you realize what they are missing.

You Might Linger to Try to Satisfy Your Cravings

Let's say that you are a drug addict, a sex addict, or perhaps an alcoholic. You see your welcomers waiting as you leave your body, but then you realize – Aha! Now you can have your fun and nobody can stop you. As grotesque as it seems, this happens, and it is a nightmare because like other earthbounds, these people soon lose their ability to perceive another reality. Without physical bodies it is impossible for them to satisfy material cravings, so these poor souls are condemned to hang hungrily in alleyways and bar rooms and bedrooms for a bleak eternity. A colorful account that I have read more than once is of a pile of naked dead people trying to copulate with one another. There is evidence that these desperate souls can possess the bodies of living addicts, which is a big reason (if you need another one) why being addicted to anything is not a good idea.

You Might Suffer an Unplanned Reincarnation

Ian Stevenson found more than two thousand children who remembered having died violent deaths and whose previous personalities could be authenticated. Debunkers can fuss that maybe he didn't follow this or that preferred protocol, but golly, when a three-year-old can go into a village where she has never been and enter a particular house and dig up coins and name relatives and in other ways prove extensive knowledge of a recently-dead person's life, then what other explanation than reincarnation can there be? Some of these children have between-lives memories of having lingered at a death scene and later entered the fetus of a passing pregnant woman, which seems to be what happens in these unusual situations. It is unclear what happens to the minds of the fetuses being taken over. Perhaps they either withdraw or share the body with the interloper, which would make this a form of spirit possession.

Most of Stevenson's cases occurred in India or Lebanon, perhaps because those societies accept the concept of reincarnation so toddlers' past-life stories were taken seriously. It may be, though, that being knocked violently from our bodies anywhere on earth can predispose us to a panicked inability to perceive our rescuers. Eventually, we may then come to believe that our only option is to enter a new fetus and start over.

You Might Suffer an Unplanned Death

A Native American prayer contains the words "protect me from unexpected death," which turns out to be a good precaution. Evidence suggests that before we are born, most of us plan into our lives several possible death events that our higher consciousness can choose to take, but an unplanned accidental death can happen. Most accident victims are found and rescued pretty quickly, but sometimes a newly dead person finds himself all alone by a swimming pool or beside the wreckage of a car. If this happens to you, call for help! Those who have been there say that help arrived as soon as they called for it, and they even say that their mother or the Angel of Light apologized for not getting there sooner.

You Might Have Strong Opinions About
What Happens at Death

One of the surest ways for people to give themselves unnecessary delays is to insist on a certain kind of after-death reality. This sort of detour seems strange at first, but once you have a better understanding of the tremendous powers of your mind, you realize how it could happen. We can almost make the blanket statement that it is better to die knowing nothing more than that happiness awaits you. Otherwise, the more certain you are about the nature of the afterlife, the more likely it is that your mind will start to generate its own reality, and you will gravitate toward other people whose illusions about heaven or hell match your own. There, believe it or not, you will find an after-death reality that looks like what you believe, but in fact it is an illusion within the larger after-death illusion.

Robert Monroe called these places hollow heavens. They seem to exist at a lower-middle level, something like Level Two or Three. People who expect to land in an afterlife that looks like a hollow heaven may peel off from their rescuers before they reach the Summerland and go there instead. These places exist outside the usual post-death process, so those who wind up in hollow heavens won't enjoy the Summerland's pleasures. Instead, they

89

exist like earthbounds in a timeless limbo. They might not find anyone they know, which pains them because they assume this means that everyone they love is in hell.

There may be many hollow heavens, but the two most often described are clouds which can include Saint Peter's Gates and a steepled church with a village around it. We are told that those who arrive in these places are glad to find that it all looks familiar. But the light is dim, and the routine they find on the cloud or in the village is so boring that it begins to feel like nobody's idea of heaven. Rescuers keep trying to get their attention. While at first these people resist the notion that there could be something better, eventually one by one they leave (further confusing those they leave behind) to join the loved ones waiting for them.

You Might Believe That Your Rescuers Are Demons

There are some religions which teach their believers that if anything happens after their deaths other than what they have been taught to expect, then it is the work of the devil. The devil is a trickster and a deceiver; he can appear as your mother or your cat or Yeshua. So rather than happily following whoever meets them at their death scene, these people shy away in fear. Some of them will become earthbound, but others will find their own hollow heavens. Either way, they are hard to rescue since no matter what their rescuers say to them and no matter how they look, these suspicious people still consider them demons.

You Might Expect to Sleep Until the Final Trumpet

There are people whose religions teach that when they die, they will fall asleep until they hear a final trumpet, and that is exactly what they do. Hospitals in the Summerland are full of sleeping or half-asleep people whose caregivers patiently try to wake them up. Finally, if nothing else will work, somebody will blow a trumpet.

You Might Have Killed Yourself

Suicide may be as bad as homicide. From a post-death perspective the chance to live and learn on earth is seen as God's gift, and when you kill yourself, you throw that gift away. People dying in pain who kill themselves generally forgive themselves easily. Children and young adults also seem able to avoid much suicide guilt. But often people who have killed themselves because they couldn't face some earth-issue are ravaged by tremendous remorse. I have read accounts by suicides that explain how they were able to forgive themselves; and other accounts of suicides for whom self-forgiveness was impossible, so they ended up on the outer-darkness level. As with everything else that we might once have regarded as sin, the problem with suicide is not the deed itself, but rather it is the added burden of guilt that suicide brings. Don't even think about killing yourself. The problem with killing yourself is that you cannot kill your mind.

You Might Not be Able to Forgive Yourself

Evidence tells us that learning to forgive is a main reason for our lives on earth, so it makes sense that failing to learn this lesson can land us in a pot of trouble. I cannot recall reading about anyone who after death failed to forgive others, but there are some harrowing accounts of the outer-darkness torment of people who were unable to forgive themselves. It appears that many of those on the lowest level never even made it to the Summerland levels. They left earth feeling guilty or evil and therefore worthy of punishment, and they promptly parted from their rescuers and put themselves into outer-darkness misery. This risk of detouring into self-punishment is such that if you do nothing else, it is crucially important that you get past any sense of personal guilt or unworthiness and feel good about yourself at your death.

Let's first set the scene here. By every account that I have read, the lowest after-death level is cold and dark and smelly and full of tormented, demon-like people sitting glumly or wailing in pain or grimly trying to do each other in. Think midnight on a garbage-dump in winter with ravening dogs around you. There are accounts of lower-level visits by Summerland folks who are recently dead, almost as if it were a tourist stop; and every such account includes an advanced guide who protected the tourist every minute. Still, as awful as it is, the outer darkness is full of spiritually advanced beings who are patiently, lovingly trying to reach and comfort each lost soul.

I do not believe that I have ever read of direct contact made through a medium with someone stuck on the outer-darkness level, although a few accounts have said that a person being sought by living loved ones is in the lowest level now and everything is being done to reach him.

Making contact is tough. We are told that most of these poor creatures cannot see or hear their rescuers; or if they notice them, they grimly shut them out. But eventually, one by one, some glimmer of something might dawn in them. Then slowly, once that contact is made, they can choose to start on a patient self-forgive-ness road toward the levels above. One account that I read years ago was from someone who had managed to reach an uncle (I think it was). She was glad to report to her living relatives that at last he had moved from his hut to a hovel where there was a bit of light. He was feeling a little better now and beginning the hard work of healing.

Never have I seen any evidence that the people in the outer darkness are put there by anyone but themselves. Some of us forgive ourselves more easily than others do, so some of the most desolate wretches on the outer-darkness level may seem to us to have done less harm than others who have escaped their fate. A story about Adolf Hitler is an example. I have seen Hitler mentioned only once, so I share this just as a story, but it seems to fit with the logic of the place. I read that Hitler was able to forgive himself without much delay, perhaps because most of the harm that he ordered was done by his underlings. But many who carried out the Holocaust have put themselves into horrendous torment. One guard is said to have locked himself in an iron box from which his wails can be heard. All the while, some of his victims cluster around his box as rescuers, imploring him to realize that everyone has forgiven him and begging him to forgive himself.

Living with Awareness

Knowing for certain that your life never ends changes everything. Having been a devout Christian all my life, I am amazed to see how much better my new certainty is than the deepest faith, and knowing so much about the afterlife trumps all my old belief in a generic heaven. Fear of death seems to be the base fear, so when you lose your fear of death, you lose your other fears as well. You even lose that old quick anger at trivial slights (and even at the big things). Now, when I am cut off in traffic, I smile and take it as the lesson in love and forgiveness that it always was. Still, even this immortal confidence and this amazing loss of fear and rage are not the primary benefit of finally knowing the truth about death.

No, the main benefit that awaits you when you know the truth about death is an extraordinary core-deep happiness. What awaits you is fun in all you do now, even before your after-death fun begins. Knowing the truth turns what life is for some – a series of tragedies in this vale of tears – into one joyful afternoon romp watched over by that ultimate Parent Who soon will call us in for hugs and kisses and supper forevermore.

Learning to live so that when we die we can have the most possible eternal fun is an exercise worth the effort later, and it pays great dividends now. Fortunately, the rules seem simple....

CHAPTER TEN

LIVING SO YOUR DYING CAN BE THE MOST FUN

"Why do you call me 'Lord, Lord,'
and do not do what I say?"
Yeshua (LK 6:46)

"Not everyone who says to me, 'Lord, Lord,' will enter
the kingdom of heaven, but only he who does the
will of my Father who is in heaven."
Yeshua (MT 7:21)

"Do not judge, and you will not be judged.
Do not condemn, and you will not be condemned.
Forgive, and you will be forgiven."
Yeshua (LK 6:37)

"You have heard that it was said, 'Love your neighbor
and hate your enemy.' But I tell you: love your
enemies and pray for those who persecute you, that
you may be sons of your Father in heaven ... Be
perfect, therefore, as your heavenly Father is perfect."
Yeshua (MT 5:43-48)

*P*eople who study afterlife evidence are struck repeatedly by the extent to which the way we live our lives on earth affects our post-death happiness. This chapter is not about morality, although it may turn out to read that way. These rules are not an admonition that we be good for goodness's sake, but instead they are more like scientific principles in a reality governed by Consciousness. As basic as the temperature at which water freezes and as implacable as gravity's tug, afterlife evidence tells us that the purpose of our earth-lives is this: we are here to learn to love each other perfectly and to learn to forgive completely. Seems simple, doesn't it? Simple it is, until we try to apply it to our lives.

Forgiving

For most of us, forgiving is a score-keeping detail in the competitive game of life. We might forgive some people but not others. We might forgive those we love but forever hold grudges against a clown at work or a jerk who stiffed us or a notorious mass-murderer. We might forgive if we get something in exchange, or we might forgive so we can feel superior to those who cannot forgive as well as we can. But evidence suggests that none of this is the sort of forgiveness that is expected of us. Indeed, I suspect that none of it is useful when our judgment day arrives.

Remember that what we are talking about is learning to flex our forgiveness muscle. When at our judgment we are put into the shoes of all the people we knew in life, and when we are made to see how much our forgiving them from the heart matters, evidence suggests that even the grumpiest of us will forgive everyone who ever wronged us. No problem. It is forgiving ourselves that is the tough part! What is needed when we face a life review is a habit of reflexive wholehearted sympathy honed in our lifelong forgiveness of others. Unless we have learned by the time we die to forgive every-one automatically, we are going to find it hard to forgive ourselves.

If earth-life is our kindergarten, then let's at least try to learn to stack our blocks right.

The sort of forgiveness that we should be learning is not what you and I might see as normal forgiveness after all. It is more like never noticing a wrong in the first place. Just as we would want a judge to see things entirely from our perspective and in our favor, so that is how we should be learning to forgive immediately each smallest slight. And even each terrible life-changing harm.

A thorough treatise on learning to forgive is far beyond the scope of this book, but as our need to learn to forgive begins to be more widely known, a forgiveness-teaching industry is bound to spring up eventually. Meanwhile, here are three tips:

1. The best source of forgiveness lessons that I know is an esoteric three-in-one volume called *A Course in Miracles*. I express no opinion about whether the author who dictated this work is Yeshua, but as a student who began the *Course* as a skeptic, I think it is the best book in print on the sort of radical forgiveness that we are supposed to be learning. If you don't now have the time that doing the whole *Course* would require, you might begin with Gary Renard's *The Disappearance of the Universe* (2002) and *Your Immortal Reality* (2006). You will have to get past the claimed source of his books, but their teachings are consistent with the *Course* and helpful.

2. Since evidence tells us that after your death you are going to forgive everyone in your life, you may as well make a habit of

forgiving everyone in your life right now. And because evidence also tells us that after your death, you are going to have to face and forgive every harm that you have done to others, you may as well beginning today make a careful habit of never harming anyone. Few of us are innately evil, so most of the harm that we do is unintentional. Now that you know how much your harming others causes harm to yourself, it is time to make yourself stop doing it.

3. Remember that you have no secrets. As Yeshua says, "There is nothing concealed that will not be disclosed, or hidden that will not be made known." (MT: 10:26) So develop a habit starting today of never thinking the smallest thought that you would mind seeing plastered in a word-bubble over your face on a Times Square billboard.

Do things right from now on. It never is too late to start.

When you realize that you are here to learn to forgive, you will start to see your life as a wonderful obstacle course of forgiveness opportunities. Watch yourself navigate the next few days and notice your reactions to people and you will see what I mean. From panhandlers to annoying brothers-in-law to cranky spouses to irritating bosses to politicians to international villains, life is a cornucopia of forgiveness lessons! When you see it as no more than that, and when you care enough about your after-death fun to want to get these lessons right, then learning to forgive becomes easier.

Loving

Learning to love spouses, family, and friends is not the point of our lives. Everyone does that. No, the kind of love that we are meant to be learning is love for those that we might think of as the most unlovable. As Yeshua says, "If you love those who love you, what reward will you get? Are not even the tax collectors doing that? And if you greet only your brothers, what are you doing more than others? Do not even pagans do that?" (MT 5:46-47)

Fortunately, it turns out that loving is a lot more fun than forgiving. Loving everyone is a form of happy-think that feels better and better the more you do it; and the more you do it, the easier it becomes. Watch for examples of extraordinary loving, like Mother Theresa of Calcutta and people who risk their lives for strangers, and ponder such things whenever you see them. Hold them in your mind as models. Practice looking at each perfect stranger and realizing that she is working on the same lessons you are, and he is a powerful eternal being. Never forget that each of the billions of people living now all over the earth is, together with you, a part of Consciousness. Essentially, literally, we all are one. Try it. Keep at it. Turns out that loving comes naturally.

I once read an account of a woman who had managed to do one anonymous good deed every day of her adult life; and if she was discovered, that deed didn't count, so she found a way to do something else. We are told that when she arrived in the Summerland, she was surprised to find herself a celebrated hero there like almost no one else before or since. Forget your 401(k)! If you want to save for your best eternal retirement, then begin today to take advantage of every lucky chance you find to do good things for other people. You can follow that woman's sterling example, but anonymity may not be so important. What seems to count most from an eternal perspective is the happiness that you give to others. And making others happy will make you happy, too, since doing good for others stimulates the same pleasure-centers of the brain that are stimulated when we do good things for ourselves. These earth-bodies are literally hard-wired to give us joy when we help others!

The best lessons in love that I have found are the words of Yeshua in the Gospels. Whether or not you are a Christian, just reading the red letters on love and forgiveness in any modern red-letter Bible may be the easiest way to get a sense of the sort of universal love and forgiveness that we are supposed to be learning.

Other Lessons

There are hints that some of us on earth are working on other and more complex lessons, but I have no idea what they might be. It seems that for most of us, learning the right way to love and forgive the rest of humanity is hard enough.

The point is that each of us should be living our lives with a lot more attention to love and forgiveness than we ever thought was necessary. We are so busy trying to make money and find a little enjoyment in life that we think of loving and forgiving as niceties. But what we learn from studying afterlife evidence is that money and the objects that we spend our lives chasing actually are the frivolous details. The things that matter in life – the only things! – are learning to love perfectly and learning to forgive completely.

Please begin with me. If in writing this book I have stepped on your particular beliefs, I ask that you forgive me and accept this book as the gift made in love that it is meant to be. Having spent my life learning what happens at death, I could not bear the thought that the truth might any longer be hidden from you.

Daring to Investigate Dying

I have come to see only recently that my studying death carried risk. What if the death-related evidence had turned out to be inconsistent nonsense? What if I had found no suggestion that my life has any meaning at all, and instead it was more than likely that the death of my brain would result in my extinction? I was so certain when I began this research that my experiences of light had been real events that the risks involved in studying death did not occur to me at the time. And now those risks seem laughable. What happens at death turns out to be far better than all my religion-inspired hopes, and still we know so little about the wonders of the afterlife. Part of the fun of coming this far and at last knowing the truth about death is realizing that beyond that door are many more unimaginable truths. Our fun of learning and growth goes on forever!

Of course, for now it is good to know that the earth is not flat after all and the sea contains no dragons. But having finally learned these truths, let us begin now to work together to better understand this ultimate new world.

APPENDIX I

TWO SUGGESTED STUDY GUIDES

You may find this book hard to believe until you have done some of your own research. Fortunately, afterlife-related evidence is abundant now and widely available, and if you want some personal pointers, the books suggested here are some of my favorites. Everyone who has an obsessive hobby is unable to believe that others don't share it, but you may already have your own hobbies, so if you want to cut to the chase, I will first give you four central resources. Read only these, and then go back to living your life with the glorious understanding that it will never end. Or if you find that you have more time, the second part of this Appendix is a more extensive guide where I can welcome you into sharing my passion.

FOUR KEY RESOURCES

The first two books given here summarize the current afterlife science for non-scientists. The third book is the most complete account of the Summerland that I have yet found; and the fourth, despite its age, is the best advice ever given for successful living. All four are brief and easy to understand and a lot of fun to read, so please read them and then go on with my love to enjoy your best possible life.

1. *Your Eternal Self* (2008) – R. Craig Hogan has written a wonderful and easily read summary of the afterlife-related science. His book is the best place to begin.

2. *Quantum Enigma* (2006) - Bruce Rosenblum and Fred Kuttner have so much fun with the physics of consciousness that they have done what I would have thought would be impossible.

They have written an enjoyable physics page-turner.

3. *Life in the World Unseen* (1993 edition) – Robert Hugh Benson through Anthony Borgia wrote the most extensive and overall accurate description of how the Summerland looks to a new arrival that I have yet read. This book may be a novel, or it may in fact have been channeled through a friend by a British Catholic priest who died in 1914. It doesn't matter. So many of the details of this book are so consistent with the briefer accounts from other sources that we have received in myriad ways that it is genuine in the only way that counts: it rings true. When you read this book, keep in mind its age and the fact that your perspective and your experiences are going to differ from Monsignor Benson's. Still, he does an excellent job of setting the afterlife stage for us.

4. *The Bible's Four Gospels* – Matthew, Mark, Luke and John have preserved for us the 2000-year-old words of someone who told us details about reality, death and the afterlife that we could not have learned through other means until the 20th century. Whether or not you are a Christian, buy a Bible that prints the words of Yeshua in red letters. Read what he says about loving and forgiving and how we should be living our lives a couple of times a week, until you start to know his words by heart. Then live by them. You have nothing to lose, and a happier life to gain both now and forevermore.

These four works will give you some of the best current information about what makes eternal life possible, what the afterlife is like, and how to make the most of this lifetime so you can have your best eternal life. Perhaps that will be enough. If it is, just let me add that if you ever have questions, you can contact us at *www. FunofDying.com* and we will do what we can to find your answers.

A MORE EXTENSIVE STUDY GUIDE

If reading these four preliminary works only whets your appetite for learning, or if they cannot quite convince you, then here are fifty-odd other books that I have enjoyed and found useful. I have listed them in categories that will make sense to someone fresh from having read *The Fun of Dying*. The books listed here are by no means the only or necessarily the best books on these subjects, nor is everything that they will tell you entirely supported by other evidence. But these books are genuine and useful, and I have read them recently enough to be able to recommend them to you.

I. The Nature of Reality

The books and CD set listed here are great background, and I urge you to read at least the first two books before you go on to read in other categories.

Your Eternal Self (2008) – In the first of our four key resources, R. Craig Hogan summarizes so much of the evidence about what is going on in such an easy and enjoyable volume that I have bought dozens of copies as gifts.

The Biology of Belief (2005) – Bruce Lipton is a cell biologist who got off the mainstream science reservation and never looked back. Like Hogan's book, Lipton's is so fundamental that it should be one of the first things you read as you get your feet wet in doing wider research. Lipton also recorded a CD set called *The Wisdom of Your Cells* that makes a great companion to his book.

Is There Life After Death? – Elisabeth Kübler-Ross was a physician who specialized in death and dying, and this CD story of her personal journey – told in her own wonderfully-accented voice – is compelling. If you don't make the time to listen to Kübler-Ross, your life will forever be the poorer for it.

The Secret Life of Plants (1972) – Forty years ago, Peter Tompkins and Christopher Bird wrote such an extraordinary book that I am amazed that so few people have heard of it. It is a long book and not directly on point, but if you have the time, please read it. I read this book when it was first published, and even today I wince a little when I cut a tomato or grate a carrot.

II. Consciousness as the Source of Reality

The conclusion that Consciousness is the source of reality will come to you only gradually, as you read more and more death-related evidence and you realize there is no other explanation. If you want to speed up the process, here are seven very different books, three of them by physicists, which should get you there more quickly.

Quantum Enigma (2006) - Bruce Rosenblum and Fred Kuttner are adventurous academic physicists, and in this second of our four key resources they give us a summary of their understanding of the consciousness issue in quantum physics. This book is plainly written and highly accessible for non-physicists, so you ought to begin your physics study here.

The Self-Aware Universe (1995) - Amit Goswami is a physicist who understands many of the implications of quantum theory. His book is a little tough for non-physicists, and because it takes into account only Eastern religious teachings, it can be a struggle for the rest of us to grasp. Still, it is fascinating support for the fundamental truth that Consciousness is all there is.

The Physics of Consciousness (2000) - Evan Harris Walker was another physicist. He is said to have been the founder of the modern science of consciousness research, and although he tries to simplify the physics, his book can be a tough slog in spots. Still, I loved every mind-bending minute of it. Walker died in August of 2006. After more than fifty years apart, he is again with Merilyn, the love of his life who died when they were both sixteen, and (his dedication says) "without whom there would be nothing."

The Unobstructed Universe (1940) - Stewart Edward White worked in the 1930s. You will be astonished to find that seventy years ago he was writing about consciousness as the source of reality and the indestructibility of consciousness and so much else! There are few books so basic. You will enjoy both him and his psychic/spirit wife, although you may find this book (if at all) only in a sixty-plus-year-old paperback.

Our Unseen Guest (1920) - Darby and Joan (pseudonyms) worked with Stephen (also a pseudonym), a soldier killed in World War I, and ninety years ago they published a seminal account which identifies consciousness as the source of reality. The first half of their book is an insightful study of the problems inherent in communicating through mediums. The second half is the earliest reasonably accurate account of reality that I have yet found. I feel about this book very much as I felt when I realized how completely modern evidence agrees with the teachings of Yeshua: if they got it right so long ago, then Darby and Joan both reinforce and are reinforced by what the evidence now tells us. And eventually when some physicist is acclaimed as the father of a consciousness theory of everything, he ought at least to acknowledge the fact that plucky young Stephen was there long before.

The Conscious Universe (1997); *Entangled Minds* (2006) - Dean Radin is an academic parapsychologist whose interest lies in the workings of psychic phenomena in a quantum reality. Dubbed by some "the Einstein of consciousness research," he never quite says that everything springs from consciousness. But his books are filled with evidence of the primary role of consciousness, and they are well done and fascinating reading.

III. The Nature of Your Mind

If you have trouble grasping the fact that your brain does not generate your mind, here are some books to help you better understand what and where your mind is, and also how powerful it is. Like it or not, the reality you create is your own!

Your Eternal Self (2008) - R. Craig Hogan makes our list again. His book is easy to read, and it is a good summary of some of the best evidence currently available. If you have managed to get to this point without having read his book, please do that now.

The Holographic Universe (1991) - Michael Talbot's master-work remains a classic in this field. Much more evidence has been developed in the two decades since this author published and soon thereafter died young, but his book remains one of the most important resources on this subject.

The Field (2001) - Lynne McTaggart is a very important pioneer in this area. Her book is indispensable background, and she also recorded two wonderful CD sets called *The Field* and *Living the Field* if you would rather listen than read.

The Divine Matrix (2007) - Gregg Braden is another major pioneer in helping us to understand where and what our minds really are, and his book is fascinating and highly readable.

IV. Near-Death Experiences (NDEs)

Most of those who have near-death experiences will spend so little time beyond the veil that generally they don't see a lot, so the primary value of their stories is the plain assurance that people pass through death with their minds intact. A few NDEs are more extensive, however, and they validate in every detail what we have learned about dying and its aftermath from other sources. One advantage of NDEs for researchers is that they have been so extensively studied for so many years that if they were not real events we would have figured that out by now. If you want to start your investigation of dying on well-trod ground, then you might begin by reading P.M.H. Atwater and Jeffrey Long.

Evidence of the Afterlife (2010) - Jeffrey Long with Paul Perry recently published what is billed as the largest study of near-death experiences ever conducted. It focuses on statistical compilations of many experiences gleaned through their website, and it also shows

109

how common NDE details (like the fact that those blind from birth are able to see during NDEs) help to prove the reality that people survive their deaths. Long and Perry claim that their book "reveals proof of life after death," and if you need to see such proof before you venture ahead then this book is for you.

Beyond the Light (Revised Edition – 2009) - P.M.H. Atwater had three NDEs in 1977, and she spent the next thirty years investigating the phenomenon. NDEs are highly variable from individual to individual, but they are consistent across cultures and they point in even small details to the same afterlife realities that we encounter in other ways. The fact that infants and young children have the same experiences that adults do (except that they don't have unpleasant NDEs) helps to prove that NDEs are more than just suggestion-induced fantasies. Atwater has written more than a dozen good books, including the enormous and daunting ***The Big Book of Near-Death Experiences*** (2007), but this one seems to be the best for our purposes.

Life After Life (1975); ***The Light Beyond*** (1988) - Raymond A. Moody, Jr., is the first popularizer of near-death experiences, and by now he is something of a legend. The experiences that he describes are commonly reported by people who attend a lot of deaths.

Ordered to Return (originally published as ***My Life After Dying***, 1991) - George G. Richie, Jr., had what may be the most elaborately detailed near-death experience ever, and his brief book is a classic in this field. Moody calls it "the best such book in print."

V. Deathbed Visions

Less well known today than near-death experiences are deathbed visions, even though they appear to be a nearly universal part of dying. All of the books listed here are enjoyable and fascinating, and I suggest that you read at least one of them.

Death-Bed Visions (1926) - Sir William Barrett wrote what remains the classic work on deathbed visions, and his brief book is a wonderful read. Unfortunately, though, it is long out of print and it may be hard to find. Reading it made me see how sad it is that today most dying people are so well sedated that they (and we) miss some wonderful experiences during the moments that they spend in two realities.

At the Hour of Death (1977) - Karlis Osis and Erlendur Haraldsson detailed a study of some 50,000 terminally ill patients observed just before their deaths by a thousand doctors and nurses in the United States and India. Osis and Haraldsson were able to rule out medical explanations for these patients' before-death visions, and they showed us that these experiences are much the same in both cultures.

One Last Hug Before I Go (2000) - Carla Wills-Brandon's summary of modern deathbed visions and other before-death and at-death phenomena is a worthy successor to Sir William's pioneering volume. It was this book that helped me understand why it is that deathbed visions may be necessary.

VI. The Design and Functioning of Extra-Material Realities

Our biggest problem in studying the realities that we enter at death is that we must get our information from fallible human beings. Whether they speak from beyond the veil, or like Bob Monroe they only visited the extra-material realities and returned, our reporters often know little more than we know, believe it or not. This means that it is very important to read many after-death accounts, since the more of them we read, the more we can see that each is giving us a slightly different miniscule glimpse of what is the same set of after-death realities.

The Place We Call Home – Exploring the Soul's Existence After Death (2000) - Robert J. Grant gives a brief and lucid examination of the extra-material realities based primarily on the Edgar Cayce materials. I have some concerns about relying on Cayce because some of his predictions have been wrong. (Actually, my studies suggest legitimate reasons for his errors, but a treatise on Cayce is, like so much else, beyond the scope of this book.) Because what Grant reports is reasonably consistent with other more esoteric sources, his book may be a good introduction.

Journeys Out of the Body (1971); *Far Journeys* (1985); *Ultimate Journey* (1994) - Robert Monroe was a successful businessman with an interesting hobby. At about age 40 he learned how to leave his physical body whenever he liked and travel in extra-material realities. A bright and ruthlessly honest researcher, he wrote three books which together present a gripping story of his own development. Monroe's books detail these realities from the viewpoint of someone who has not died, and therefore he was not protected in his travels as you and I will be at death. From his out-of-body perspective we see less of the scenery and more of the scaffolding. What is interesting about his books to me is the fact that nevertheless Monroe describes essentially the same beyond-death realities as what we discover from other sources. His perspective lets us better appreciate how lovingly the post-death process is designed to protect and nurture each of us.

Cosmic Journeys (1999) - Rosalind A. McKnight was one of Monroe's Explorers, the volunteers who replicated his out-of-body work under laboratory conditions. Her book describes her experiences as a naïve and untrained but fearless participant. The first part is a bit silly, but the second half is great, and the view of reality that she sets forth here is amply corroborated elsewhere.

After We Die, What Then? (1987); *Enjoy Your Own Funeral* (1999) - George W. Meek spent his retirement studying the after-death realities. His books are easy and enjoyable reads, and they contain useful diagrams of the upper levels and the nesting of your various bodies – so long as you always remember that all the levels and bodies exist in about the same place (to the extent that talking about "place" means anything). Meek was an important Instrumental Transcommunication (ITC) and Electronic Voice Phenomena (EVP) pioneer, so his books also contain interesting sections on these topics.

Journey of Souls (1994); *Destiny of Souls* (2000) - Michael Newton hypnotically regressed a number of people in deep trance to what they said were their lives between lives, and he reported in two books what they told him. After having read many afterlife stories, I was astonished to read these books and find that the accounts that they contained were different from most of the others. They seemed oddly impersonal, even mechanical, although the after-death process that they described was consistent with what I had found elsewhere. It was only later that I thought about the possibility that when we are under deep hypnosis, we may be accessing our eternal minds rather than the more limited minds of the individuals who have just died. If that is true, then these books are interesting for that fact alone. Most of what they say is reasonably consistent with other evidence, although they also contain some things that I have not been able to corroborate. These shouldn't be the first books on this topic that you read, but later on if you are curious and open-minded you might enjoy them.

Our Unseen Guest (1920); ***The Unobstructed Universe*** (1940) - Darby and Joan and Stewart Edward White were colleagues nearly a century ago, and the two books listed here are the earliest reasonably accurate modern summaries of afterlife details that I have yet found. The fact that I came across them only after I had pieced together most of this from other sources made them astounding to me, although if I had read them decades ago I might not have taken them seriously. These books are highly readable, and you will find them to be both informative and still on the cutting edge. I urge you to read them, even though you will find them only in libraries or in used paperbacks.

VII. After-Death Communications

There is such a religious and cultural stigma attached to communicating with the dead that at first I tried to ignore after-death communications. There are so many such accounts, however, and they are so consistent across communication styles and through a century and a half of stories, that I am convinced now that nearly all of those available in print are genuine. You ought to read as many as you can, since it is impossible to learn about the afterlife where these folks reside unless we are willing to listen to their descriptions. I will list a few of my favorites by category, but before you read them you might read about Gary Schwartz's work, which provides some scientific validation for afterlife communications.

The Afterlife Experiments (2002) - Gary E. Schwartz used traditional scientific methods to study psychic mediums with remarkable success. In my experience, many professional mediums pick up cues from us and provide suspiciously general information; and even talented mediums may have trouble talking with your own dead relatives (most of whom have better things to do now than trying to get through to you). There, I've said it: using mediums to contact your dead relatives is among the worst ways to attempt a general study of non-material realities. Still, there are some psychic mediums who have amply proven their powers, and Schwartz's book will help you better appreciate what they can do.

Hello From Heaven! (1995) - Bill Guggenheim and Judy Guggenheim wrote the pioneering book on personal After-Death Communications (ADCs). Often the closest survivors of those who are recently dead will experience communications, some of them spectacular. Indeed, it has been estimated that close to half of widows and widowers see a vision of the departed spouse within the first year. The Guggenheims interviewed some 2000 people and collected and categorized more than 3,300 accounts of their ADC experiences. This book has become a classic.

VIII. ITC and EVP

Instrumental Transcommunication (ITC) and Electronic Voice Phenomena (EVP) are in their infancy, but they show a lot of promise. After all, who needs an unreliable medium if you can pick up the phone and have a chat with dead relatives?

Miracles in the Storm (2001); ***Spirit Faces*** (2006) - Mark Macy has been at the center of ITC and EVP research, and his books are a good introduction to these subjects. The first book listed here details how almost a decade of promising research fell apart in the late 1990s because clashes among some of the living research-ers caused their dead collaborators to withdraw. The second book includes a summary of some extra-material details gleaned from Borgia's book and two similar primary sources.

IX. Group Contacts

What is needed for real evidential contact to take place between our level of reality and the levels occupied by the dead is the sincere long-term commitment of living people to the process. The dead know who is genuine and who is not, and sometimes when they find a group that seems to them to be worth the effort, a team of the dead will begin what for them is a difficult process and use their liv-ing collaborators as a way to deliver validating evidence. The best ITC and EVP are produced this way, as are most other remarkable proofs, like apports (items materializing in air), images produced on film, and even human materializations. I have never read of a team of dead collaborators who began the process and then tired of it, but living people seldom devote the time and energy required for more than a few years. What happened in the village of Scole in Norfolk, England, in the mid-nineties is an example of the sort of wonderful result that can be obtained by dedicated researchers who are willing to let their dead collaborators take the lead.

The Scole Report (1999) - The most extensive report to date on collaborations with the dead is available as a research paper that was printed in the Proceedings of the Society for Psychical Research, Volume 58, Part 220, in November of 1999. You can find it in many university libraries, and if you resort to copying it you will want to make color copies of its wonderful illustrations. *The Scole Report* describes a scientific investigation of some extraordinary valida-tions which were visited on The Scole Experimental Group from 1993 through 1998 at Scole in Norfolk, England.

The Scole Experiment (1999) - Grant and Jane Solomon worked with The Scole Experimental Group to summarize the findings detailed in *The Scole Report* for general readers. When you read this book, be aware that the full *Scole Report* is even more wonderful.

X. Accounts Received Through Deep-Trance Mediums

The late 19th and early 20th centuries were the heyday of deep-trance mediums. What appears to be needed for talented living psychics to develop this skill is many years of passively sitting in the dark night after night, and in the days before radio, there were folks who started with fads like table-tipping and went on to become amazingly good trance mediums. Trance mediums could withdraw from their bodies and let a dead medium (called a "control") take over. These controls then spoke using the living medium's vocal cords, which was a much more fruitful process than modern-day psychic-medium mind-reading. Controls had with them dead friends and relatives of people sitting in the room, who gave such abundant evidence of their identities that it is irrational not to credit these accounts. Some deep-trance mediums were also able to channel higher-level beings. I have listed here just three accounts of the work of the same early-20th-century team. If you like these, you will find other such works available in used books and reprints.

Some New Evidence For Human Survival (1922); *Life Beyond Death With Evidence* (1928); *In the Dawn Beyond Death* (late 1930s) - Charles Drayton Thomas was a British Methodist minister who worked with a deep-trance medium named Gladys Osborne Leonard and her dead control, Feda. He was a curious and methodical fellow investigating what he saw as a cutting-edge phenomenon that was delivering world-changing information. Reading these books in order gives you a sad sense of what a lost period the whole 20th century really was. Scientists had spent the latter part of the 19th century disparaging and trying to debunk all evidence related to mental telepathy and other psi phenomena. Then the early 20th century brought a flood of afterlife communications produced through deep-trance mediums, so scientists of the day changed their tack. They began to insist that these were not communications from the dead at all, but the mediums were reading the minds of living relatives. So then some of the teams of dead collaborators who were working with deep-trance mediums set out to prove their existence to scientists by devising clever tests for themselves which would rule out the possibility of mind-reading. Thomas's 1922 book is less interesting to us than are the other two listed here because most of it is patient documentation of the results of these self-tests by the dead delivered to help scientists overcome their skepticism. The dead passed nearly all their own tests, which fact may have alarmed the scientific community. So by the time of Thomas's 1922 book, mainstream science had changed its course again and was flat ignoring any evidence that did not fit with atheism. If you have never heard of Charles Drayton Thomas and his ninety-year-old book of proofs that were given by his dead collaborators, you know that even then mainstream science's stonewalling was sadly effective.

XI. First-Person Accounts Received Through Automatic Writing

You can believe in these books or not, as you like, but there are some interesting first-person accounts by dead people who communicated through automatic writing. Someone with mediumistic ability sat with pen in hand or with fingers on the keys, and a dead person with similar abilities then wrote as if those hands were his own. The result was a book which was apparently written by a dead person. The books listed here are quick and enjoyable reads, and nearly all of what they tell us is amply corroborated elsewhere. If you can accept how they were received, they are a useful introduction to the after-death realities.

Life in the World Unseen (1993 edition); *More About Life in the World Unseen* (1956) - Robert Hugh Benson was a British Catholic priest who died in 1914 and discovered after his death that some of what he had written during his lifetime about the afterlife was wrong. So through his friend, Anthony Borgia, he wrote the first of these books, which is the third of our four key resources. I came across these books late in my research, and I found them to be so consistent with what I had already learned from other sources as to be frankly astonishing. No matter where these two volumes came from, they are useful first-person accounts of how the afterlife levels can appear to those newly arrived.

The Book of James (1974) - William James and Susy Smith wrote an entertaining book that seems to be mostly consistent with the rest of the evidence. William James, the brother of novelist Henry James, was a late-19th-century Harvard professor of psychology, and the first president of the American Society for Psychical Research. Susy Smith was a psychic and a prominent researcher during the 1970s, when this book was dictated.

Testimony of Light (1969) - Frances Banks and Helen Greaves have given us a fascinating portrayal of Banks's early adjustments to life after death. Banks was an Episcopal nun and a spiritual seeker all her life. So many of the details of her account of what happened to her after her death are so consistent with other evidence that her slim volume seems well worth reading.

XII. Reincarnation

There is so much evidence for reincarnation that clearly something like it happens. It is a difficult process to understand, however, since time is not objectively real, so somehow all our lives on earth are happening at the same time. Accounts from upper-level beings suggest that we think of reincarnation not as a linear process, but more as a vat from which the bucket of each lifetime is dipped and back into which each lifetime is poured, and that is how I have come to envision reincarnation. But who knows? If you wonder about reincarnation, here are a few good books on the subject.

Reliving Past Lives (1978) - Helen Wambach's groundbreaking study of mass hypnotic regressions is a brief and fascinating book. She set out to disprove reincarnation by hypnotically regressing thousands of people to lives lived in specific historical periods, expecting to be able to record an inconsistent mess of fantasy and gibberish. What she found instead was a distribution of thousands of memories of past lives that included genders, locations, clothing, utensils, foods, and other small details which so perfectly matched the historical record that to have achieved these results by chance was nearly mathematically impossible.

Twenty Cases Suggestive of Reincarnation (1971); ***Unlearned Language*** (1984); ***Where Reincarnation and Biology Intersect*** (1997) - Ian Stevenson was for many years Chairman of the Department of Psychiatry at the University of Virginia, and he was a leading researcher in the field of reincarnation. Stevenson spent a half-century studying cases of young children who remembered recent previous lives that ended violently, and the result is a spectacular body of work which will be celebrated only when the rest of modern science catches up with it. Stevenson wrote for scientists, so his writing style is dry. But the work that he details in his dozen or more volumes is overwhelming evidence for reincarnation in what appears to be the narrow case of unexpected violent death. These are three of his seminal works.

Many Lives, Many Masters (1988); *Same Soul, Many Bodies* (2004) - Brian Weiss is the foremost popularizer of past-life regression therapy for use in the treatment of medical and psychological problems. An eminent Yale-trained psychiatrist, Weiss accidentally discovered the effect that apparent past lives can have on our present. Unlike other regression therapists who have made the same discovery, he risked his medical career to get the word out. He has even ventured into the newer field of progression therapy (the investigation of how our future lives might affect the present one), which Consciousness theory suggests should be possible, although it is a lot harder for us linear-thinking humans to grasp. The result is two illuminating books which offer a good introduction to the whole topic of reincarnation.

Children's Past Lives (1997); *Return From Heaven* (2001) - Carol Bowman has studied the past-life memories of children, and while most of Stevenson's subjects remembered only their most recent lives, Bowman studied children whose present lives appeared to have been affected by traumas suffered in more distant lifetimes. She also has studied the phenomenon of children quickly reincarnating within the same family, which appears to happen fairly often when infants or toddlers die.

Reincarnation – The Missing Link in Christianity (1997) -
Elizabeth Clare Prophet wrote a scholarly but highly readable exposition of reincarnation as an original Christian belief. People who doubt that reincarnation was taught and believed by the earliest Christians owe it to themselves to read this book.

XIII. Spirit Possession

You may or may not take seriously something for which there is considerable evidence: it may be possible for living people to be possessed by spirits of the dead. Indeed, the condition may even be common, and it may be the cause of any number of otherwise inexplicable maladies. Who knows? Unlike mediumship and near-death experiences, possession has scarcely been studied at all, and spirit-releasement therapy is seldom practiced now because state regulators and malpractice insurers frown on it. This attitude can be expected to change once Consciousness is shown to be the source of reality. Meanwhile, those few therapists who have made their careers in spirit-releasement therapy (the process of coaxing possessing beings away from their victims and toward the loved ones waiting for them) have had such apparent success that you may find these books fascinating.

People Who Don't Know They're Dead (2005) - Gary Leon Hill wrote a quick and enjoyable book which is a useful introduction to the topic.

Healing Lost Souls (2003) - William J. Baldwin was a late-20th-century expert in this field.

XIV. Learning How to Forgive

I had known for years about *A Course in Miracles*, but it wasn't until late in my research that I came across Gary Renard's first book and realized that the *Course* appeared to fill some of the remaining gaps in my understanding. It is especially good as a set of lessons in radical forgiveness, and I recommend it to you for that purpose. Beware, though: the *Course* is heavy stuff! It is beautifully written in Elizabethan English, and the upper-level Master who channeled it (the author may have been Yeshua himself) was so determined to elevate our understanding that it can take years for students of the *Course* to begin to comprehend its teachings. The *Course* doesn't speak to the period right after death, and it uses some terms in unfamiliar ways. For example, what the *Course* calls "consciousness" is what you and I might call "personal awareness." Still, for anyone familiar with the afterlife literature, the teachings of the *Course* deeply resonate. Gary Renard claims that two advanced beings gave him some of the *Course*'s teachings in simpler form. Wherever Renard's books came from, beginning with them can make the *Course* more understandable.

The Disappearance of the Universe (2002); *Your Immortal Reality* (2006) - Gary R. Renard is, ahem, the present-day incarnation of... I guess I shouldn't give that away. Renard claims extraordinary help, and some of what he says is a stretch, but his books are fun to read. Renard also recorded a good CD set called *The End of Reincarnation,* which might be a place to start. My one quibble with his CDs is that he ventures into talking about death and reincarnation, where evidence fails to support what he says. Ignore that, and concentrate on what he has to say about forgiveness.

A Course in Miracles – Purportedly in the 1960s Yeshua dictated through Helen Schucman with the help of William Thetford a restatement and completion of his Gospel teachings. If you are ready to live your life to have the best possible time after death, and especially if your need to learn to forgive completely has been a problem, then this three-in-one book is for you. The ***Course*** is a real course of study, and heavy reading, but there are study groups all over the world that can help you with your learning and your personal growth. If you are eager to bypass most of the Summerland and arrive right at Level Four or higher, then spending the rest of your life on the ***Course*** is going to be your surest bet. Indeed, learning real forgiveness is so hard for most of us that I consider working through *A **Course** in Miracles* to be the single most useful thing that we can do to make the most of our lives.

XV. Learning How to Love

Unlike forgiving, loving is easy to learn. It seems to come naturally to most of us, and the more we love, the easier it becomes to love. For an understanding of the kind of love that evidence suggests we should be learning, and also for a pretty decent treatise on learning to forgive, what I believe is the best resource may already be on your shelf.

The Bible's Four Gospels - Matthew, Mark, Luke, and John are credited with having written the only books of the Bible which carry the words of Yeshua himself, and they are our fourth and final key resource. Historical evidence suggests that the Gospels were compiled from oral tradition and written resources beginning a few decades after Yeshua's death, and we know that in the subsequent two millennia they were edited, but they are what we have. My own current favorite Bible is a *New International Version Red-Letter Edition*, although any modern translation will do; just be sure to choose a Bible which prints the words of Yeshua in red letters. For our purposes, look only at what Yeshua has to say about loving and forgiving and how we should be living our lives. Don't look for mystical or religious meaning in what Yeshua seems to be saying. Just listen to him as you would listen to a friend who knows a great deal more than you do and is trying to help you get it right.

APPENDIX II

LISTENING TO YESHUA

Yeshua's words are amazingly consistent with afterlife-related evidence, but a lot of what mainstream Christianity teaches is not. It turns out that the dead don't sleep until they hear a final trumpet, their bodies don't reassemble out of the soil, and those who rescue them are not demons. Being baptized does not seem to matter after death, having taken communion doesn't matter, and accepting Yeshua as our personal savior seems to make no afterlife difference. Evidence suggests that practicing any religion in life does not matter after death, but what counts for us when we die is our having lived our lives in close accordance with Yeshua's Gospel teachings.

For most of my life I was a traditional Christian and frankly afraid to be anything else. Then in my late fifties I realized that Christianity was inconsistent with afterlife-related evidence, but Yeshua himself was amazingly accurate. That was when I took seriously his invitation to "Ask and it will be given to you; seek and you will find" (MT 7:7). I have no wish to change anyone's religion, so if you think that seeing another view of Yeshua might shake your faith, then please skip the rest of this Appendix. But if you are less devoted to Christianity than you are to Yeshua himself, you may be interested in seeing another perspective on his mission and his message.

It seems to me important now to give Yeshua a life in people's minds that might eventually need to become independent of mainstream Christianity. The afterlife realities are as real as this material universe, so inevitably mainstream science is going to find them sooner or later. Gradually then as scientists establish communications with the Summerland, it will become clear that Christianity has not been teaching what is factual. If as a result believers begin to turn away from Christianity, we don't want them also to turn away from Yeshua.

Reading Yeshua's Gospel Teachings

Think how extraordinary it is that we have the two-thousand-year-old words of someone who claimed to understand reality and to know what happens when we die. Now add the fact that most of what Yeshua says in the Gospels is consistent with what we can only now deduce from afterlife evidence and cutting-edge science. This gives us some amazing validation of both the teachings of Yeshua and the modern evidence! Such an extensive coincidence is so unlikely as to be for practical purposes impossible. Yet if you share my wonder and delight at finding how well the words of Yeshua fit the evidence, I have to remind you that the odds are long against our having available to us exactly what he said.

Many Christians consider the entire Bible to be the Inspired Word of God. Having read it through several times, I find the Bible to be so internally inconsistent and so full of culturally biased and even un-Christian advice that it seems presumptuous and insulting to pin it all on God. It seems more accurate to say that the writers whose work was assembled into the Christian Bible may have been inspired by God, but they heard Him through the filter of their primitive lives in the ancient world, so they could have garbled some of God's message. This would be understandable and forgivable. But the fact that it might have happened means that no serious researcher can use most of the Bible as a resource when trying to understand a factual God.

The red letters of the Bible are another matter. Thomas Jefferson said that the words of Yeshua stand out in the Bible "like diamonds in a dunghill," and when you read the Bible through and reach the Gospels, you can understand what he meant. In a recent translation, Yeshua sounds like a modern man trying to educate primitives: you see him speaking simply and patiently, saying things over and over again to people who seem not to understand him. You even see his rising frustration, and his repeated efforts to quell that frustration and say it over yet again, more simply. Put aside the fact that Yeshua's followers started in his name a prominent and now widely fragmented religion. Then read his words without religious bias, and you find yourself sympathizing and liking him as a wonderfully wise and good man you would enjoy having as your friend. Reading his words without religious bias makes you wonder whether things that he said might be found to be factually accurate.

Here is where our problems arise. If we don't want to indulge in the magic-thinking notion that the Bible is the Inspired Word of God, then we have to take into account how easily the words of Yeshua could have been distorted during the past two thousand years:

- Those who heard Yeshua speak and passed his words along and then committed them to writing seem not to have fully understood what he was saying. It is possible that they inserted or altered words or passages here and there to better support their own understandings.

- Yeshua's message could have been altered as it was translated into modern languages. Because this is a worry, I invite you to check the Gospel passages used here against the Bible edition of your choice. I have done some of this, and have found only stylistic and not meaningful differences.

- And of course we depend on the good will of those who were in control of the written Gospels for two millennia. Here is where our trust is tested! There is evidence that people eager to support their own religious doctrines edited the Gospels over the years, which means that words could have been put into or taken out of Yeshua's mouth. We would be none the wiser.

A few of Yeshua's Gospel words are lumps of coal among the diamonds. He talks about a fiery hell; he calls Peter the rock on which he will build his church. These passages are inconsistent with afterlife-related evidence and also with the rest of Yeshua's Gospel teachings, which leads me to believe that they are doctrinal edits. If we ignore these atypical bits, then what we have left in all four Gospels is a message that is stunningly consistent with modern afterlife evidence. The man clearly knew what he was talking about, since his words agree with modern evidence in ways that could not have been known – and, indeed, might not have been liked – by the people who preserved them.

Yeshua and Mainstream Christianity

Yeshua is absolutely right in light of modern evidence, but mainstream Christianity is not. Is it possible that mainstream Christianity has misunderstood the teachings of Yeshua? Might Christianity not be Yeshua's religion after all but instead a religion grounded in the Apostles, a kind of Paulianity?

Let us imagine that we are only now finding the Gospel words of Yeshua, and we know nothing about the religion that was established in his name. We can see from afterlife-related evidence that two thousand years ago, Yeshua was familiar with facts about reality and death that have come to light only recently. If all that we had were his newly found teachings, the afterlife evidence, and the afterlife science, how might we now interpret Yeshua's words?

He Taught Us About God

Yeshua told us the fundamental fact that God is loving Spirit and each of us is part of God. This was radical stuff in ancient times, when most people worshiped semi-physical gods who were more like the Old Testament's Jehovah, often vengeful and hard to placate.

> God is spirit, and his worshipers must worship in spirit and in truth. (JN 4:24)

> The kingdom of God is within you. (LK 17:21)

> The Spirit gives life; the flesh counts for nothing. The words I have spoken to you are spirit and they are life. (JN 6:63)

> I and the Father are one. (JN 10:30)

> If you love me, you will obey what I command. And I will ask the Father, and he will give you another Counselor to be with you forever – the Spirit of truth. The world cannot accept him, because it neither sees him nor knows him. But you know him, for he lives with you and will be in you.
> (JN 14:15-17)

Yeshua took the ancient Hebrews' radical new concept of a single nonphysical God, and he transformed it into what modern evidence shows us is universal Spirit (or Mind).

He Taught Us the Importance of Love

Yeshua reduced the Old Testament's Ten Commandments to one commandment: that we learn how to love.

> A new command I give you: Love one another. As I have loved you, so you must love one another.
> (JN 13:34)

> "Love the Lord your God with all your heart and with all your soul and with all your mind." This is the first and greatest commandment. And the second is like it: "Love your neighbor as yourself." All the Law and the Prophets hang on these two commandments.
> (MT 22:37-40)

> You have heard that it was said, "Love your neighbor and hate your enemy." But I tell you: love your enemies and pray for those who persecute you, that you may be sons of your Father in heaven.... Be perfect, therefore, as your heavenly Father is perfect.
> (MT 5:43-48)

He Taught Us the Importance of Forgiveness

When I first realized that God does not judge us, I worried that on this point Yeshua had been mistaken. But then I found this series of quotations.

> For if you forgive men when they sin against you, your heavenly Father will also forgive you. But if you do not forgive men their sins, your Father will not forgive your sins.
> (MT 6:14-15)

Moreover, the Father judges no one, but has entrusted all judgment
to the Son, that all may honor the Son just as they honor the Father.
(JN 5:22-23)

You judge by human standards; I pass judgment on no one.
(JN 8:15)

As for the person who hears my words but does not keep them, I
do not judge him. For I did not come to judge the world, but to
save it.
(JN 12:47)

Were these messages inconsistencies? I think not. Instead,
I think they were Yeshua's efforts to wean his primitive listeners
from their old idea of God as judge so they could better comprehend
what modern evidence tells us is true. Yeshua's disciple Peter asked
him, "Lord, how many times shall I forgive my brother when he sins
against me? Up to seven times?" Yeshua answered, "I tell you, not
seven times, but seventy-seven times." (MT 18:21-23)

Do not judge, or you too will be judged. For in the same way you
judge others, you will be judged, and with the measure you use, it
will be measured to you.
(MT 7:1-2).

He Taught Us the Need for Humility

In that ancient class-obsessed world, Yeshua brought a rude shock
for the elite: after our death, our life-status does not count.

Many who are first will be last, and the last first.
(MK 10:31)

The greatest among you will be your servant. For whoever exalts himself will be humbled, and whoever humbles himself will be exalted.
(MT 23:11-12)

Whoever welcomes this little child in my name welcomes me, and whoever welcomes me welcomes the one who sent me. For he who is least among you all – he is the greatest.
(LK 9:48)

Let the little children come to me, and do not hinder them, for the kingdom of God belongs to such as these. I tell you the truth, anyone who will not receive the kingdom of God like a little child will never enter it. (MK 10:14-15)

He Taught Us About the Nature of Our Minds

Mainstream Christian doctrines ignore something that strikes a modern nonreligious reader: Yeshua said a lot about the power of our minds to affect reality.

Take heart, daughter. Your faith has healed you.
(MT 9:22)

(healing a blind man) Do you believe that I am able to do this?... According to your faith will it be done to you.
(MT 9:28-29)

(when Peter couldn't walk on water) You of little faith. Why did you doubt?
(MT 14:31)

Who touched me? Someone touched me. I know that power has gone out from me...Daughter, your faith has healed you. Go in peace.
(LK 8:46-48)

Have faith in God. I tell you the truth, if anyone says to this mountain, "Go, throw yourself into the sea," and does not doubt in his heart but believes that what he says will happen, it will be done for him. Therefore I tell you, whatever you ask for in prayer, believe that you have received it, and it will be yours.
(MK 11:22-24)

It is difficult for us to appreciate how radical these teachings were in the Judea and Samaria of two thousand years ago. Yeshua used the familiar Hebrew concept of faith in God to teach his followers the power of their eternal minds, and to teach them that their minds – like his – were part of one universal Mind.

When you pray, go into your room, close the door and pray to your Father, who is unseen. Then your Father, who sees what is done in secret, will reward you.
(MT 6:6)

For whatever is hidden is meant to be disclosed, and whatever is concealed is meant to be brought out into the open. If anyone has ears to hear, let him hear.
(MK 4:22-23)

He Taught Us About the Afterlife

Some of the messages attributed to Yeshua seem inexplicable and even cruel until we compare them with afterlife evidence. That is when we realize that Yeshua was talking about not this life, but the life to come. Having read this book, see how much more sense these Gospel teachings make to you now.

> For everyone who has will be given more, and he will have an abundance. Whoever does not have, even what he has will be taken from him. And throw that worthless servant outside, into the darkness, where there will be weeping and gnashing of teeth.
> (MT 25:29:30)a

> For there is nothing hidden that will not be disclosed, and nothing concealed that will not be known or brought out into the open. Therefore consider carefully how you listen. Whoever has will be given more; whoever does not have, even what he thinks he has will be taken from him.
> (LK 8:17-18)

Yeshua told us about the tremendous size of the afterlife. He told us about our eternal progress. He even told us that our loved ones would create after-death homes for us and would meet us at our deaths and take us there.

> In my father's house are many rooms; if it were not so, I would have told you. I am going there to prepare a place for you. And if I go and prepare a place for you, I will come back and take you to be with me that you also may be where I am. You know the way to the place where I am going.
> (JN 14:2-4)

Blessed are the poor in spirit, for theirs is the kingdom of
heaven.... Blessed are the pure in heart, for they will see God.
(MT 5:3, 8)

His Teachings Are a Prescription for Afterlife Advancement

After our deaths, the law of spiritual advancement is implacable.
Much of what Yeshua says in the Gospels can be read as lessons in
better controlling your mind.

Do not resist an evil person. If someone strikes you on the right
cheek, turn to him the other also. And if someone wants to sue you
and take your tunic, let him have your cloak as well. If someone
forces you to go one mile, go with him two miles.
(MT 5:39-41)

You have heard that it was said to the people long ago, "Do not
murder, and anyone who murders will be subject to judgment." But
I tell you that anyone who is angry with his brother will be subject to
judgment. Again, anyone who says to his brother, "Raca," is answerable to the Sanhedrin. But anyone who says, "You fool" will be in
danger of the fire of hell.
(MT 5:21-22)

Why do you look at the speck of sawdust in your brother's eye and
pay no attention to the plank in your own eye? How can you say to
your brother, "Brother, let me take the speck out of your eye," when
you yourself fail to see the plank in your own eye? You hypocrite,
first take the plank out of your eye, and then you will see clearly to
remove the speck from your brother's eye.
(LK 6:41- 42)

If any one of you is without sin, let him be the first to throw a stone at her.
(JN 8:7)

But love your enemies, do good to them, and lend to them without expecting to get anything back. Then your reward will be great, and you will be sons of the Most High, because he is kind to the ungrateful and wicked. Be merciful, just as your Father is merciful.
(LK 6:35-36)

Yeshua also shared with his followers wonderful parables about spiritual growth. We know them as the tales of the Good Samaritan, the Keeper of the Vineyard, and the Prodigal Son. In every way that he could, he urged his listeners to keep striving for spiritual perfection.

I tell you that in the same way there is more rejoicing in heaven over one sinner who repents than over ninety-nine righteous persons who do not need to repent.
(LK 15:7)

He Did Not Like Clergymen or Religious Traditions

Yeshua was kind to everyone. He loved even lepers and tax collectors, at a time when lepers were shunned by all and tax collectors were evil incarnate. The only people who irritated him were clergymen. He was bothered by not just their fake piety and self-importance, but also their religious traditions.

Watch out for the teachers of the law. They like to walk around in flowing robes and be greeted in the marketplaces, and have the most important seats in the synagogues and the places of honor at banquets. They devour widows' houses and for a show make lengthy prayers. Such men will be punished most severely.
(MK 12:38-40)

And why do you break the command of God for the sake of your tradition?... You hypocrites! Isaiah was right when he prophesied about you: "These people honor me with their lips, but their hearts are far from me. They worship me in vain; their teachings are but rules taught by men."
(MT 15:3-9)

You have let go of the commands of God and are holding on to the traditions of men... You have a fine way of setting aside the commands of God in order to observe your own traditions!
(MK 7:8-9)

Be careful not to do your "acts of righteousness" before men, to be seen by them. If you do, you will have no reward from your Father in heaven.
　　　So when you give to the needy, do not announce it with trumpets, as the hypocrites do in the synagogues and on the streets, to be honored by men. I tell you the truth, they have received their reward in full. But when you give to the needy, do not let your left hand know what your right hand is doing, so that your giving may be in secret. Then your father, who sees what is done in secret, will reward you. When you pray, do not be like the hypocrites, for they love to pray standing in the synagogues and on the street corners to be seen by men. I tell you the truth, they have received their reward in full. When you pray, go into your room, close the door and pray to your Father, who is unseen. Then your Father, who sees what is done in secret, will reward you. (MT 6:1-6)

Does this sound like someone who was trying to establish his own religion? Or was he instead telling us that we could approach God individually, based upon his Gospel teaching that each of us is part of universal Mind? Yeshua's teachings are profoundly individual.

> Ask and it will be given to you; seek and you will find; knock and the door will be opened to you. For everyone who asks receives; he who seeks finds; and to him who knocks, the door is opened.
> (LK 11:9-10)
>
> Not everyone who says to me, "Lord, Lord," will enter the kingdom of heaven, but only he who does the will of my Father who is in heaven.
> (MT 7:21)
>
> Why do you call me "Lord, Lord," and do not do what I say?
> (LK 6:46)
>
> If you hold to my teaching, you are really my disciples. Then you will know the truth, and the truth will set you free.
> (JN 8:31-32)

It amazes me that so little has been made of the fact that this perfectly loving man seems to have had an aversion to religions. Does it not seem possible that, far from establishing yet one more religion, Yeshua was trying to "set you free" from religions altogether?

His Death May Not Have Been Meant to Save Us

I have a confession to make. I have always found it hard to believe that an infinitely loving God could demand the blood-sacrifice of His own child. Whenever I asked clergymen about it, I would be told it was "a sacred mystery." However, afterlife evidence tells us that accepting Yeshua as one's personal savior is not necessary for salvation, and neither God nor any religious figure is our afterlife judge. So if Yeshua didn't die as a blood-sacrifice to redeem us from God's punishment for our sins, then what else might have been the purpose of his dramatic death and resurrection?

Perhaps it was an exclamation point. Perhaps he was demonstrating for simple people the good news that death is not real.

Yeshua's Message Is Not That Being Christian Is the Only Way to Salvation

As Christianity developed, Christians became convinced that Yeshua had said that accepting him as one's personal savior was the only way to heaven.

> I am the way, the truth and the life. No one comes to the Father
> except through me.
> (JN 14:6)

> I am the resurrection and the life. He who believes in me will live,
> even though he dies; and whoever lives and believes in me will never
> die.
> (JN 11:25-26)

Afterlife evidence does not support this Christians-only reading of his words, but it would support another reading. Simply replace "I" and "me" with "my teachings":

"My teachings are the way, the truth and the life. No one comes to the Father except through my teachings."

"My teachings are the resurrection and the life. He who believes in my teachings will live, even though he dies; and whoever lives and believes in my teachings will never die."

Yeshua so persistently emphasized our need to follow his *teachings* that this revised reading makes more sense. Perhaps those who heard him misunderstood him, or perhaps later custodians of his words altered them to better support developing Christian doctrines. Unfortunately, though, in reliance on those altered words, Yeshua's followers soon were torturing and murdering and committing mayhem in his name, in utter contravention of his teachings. No conversion effort has been too brutal to be used, if making people Christian is the only way to "save" them.

But Yeshua told us repeatedly that following his *teachings* is what matters!

> What do you think? There was a man who had two sons. He went to the first and said, "Son, go and work today in the vineyard." "I will not," he answered, but later he changed his mind and went. Then the father went to the other son and said the same thing. He answered, "I will, sir," but he did not go. Which of the two did what his father wanted?... I tell you the truth, the tax collectors and the prostitutes are entering the kingdom of God ahead of you.
> (MT 21:28-31)

> I say to you that many will come from the east and the west, and will take their places at the feast with Abraham, Isaac and Jacob in the kingdom of heaven. But the subjects of the kingdom will be thrown outside, into the darkness, where there will be weeping and gnashing of teeth.
> (MT 8:11-12)

Most comforting of all his words are these: "I shall be with you always, to the very end of the age." (MT 28:20)

What Was His Mission?

Yeshua was speaking to primitive people steeped in superstitious terrors and ignorant of nearly everything that you and I consider commonplace. His teachings for them were simple, even simplistic.

We severely underestimate the man if we suppose that if he walked the earth today he would express himself to us as he expressed himself to them. If we keep this fact in mind, then in light of modern afterlife evidence, we can develop a pretty good sense of what Yeshua was trying to do.

I think that Yeshua's life had a four-fold purpose. First, he came to tell us what God is. Second, he came to show us that life is eternal. Third, he came to give us a taste of what the afterlife is like. Finally, he came to teach us how to make the most spiritual progress while on earth. Human beings were ready to start to learn what modern afterlife evidence has only now revealed to us, two very bloody millennia later. Had his followers fully understood what he was saying at the time, human history could have been so different!

Mainstream Christianity does not own Yeshua, just as no religion owns God. Surely he deserves another chance to be heard in light of modern afterlife evidence. Paul and the other New Testament writers did a good job of wrapping Yeshua's teachings in Hebrew prophesy so they could be preserved for two thousand years. Thank you, Paul. Now it may be time to open your gift.

APPENDIX III

EXPERIENCES OF LIGHT

My interest in death is an offshoot of something that happened in April of 1955. One morning I woke up just before dawn and realized that there is no God. I stared in terror into the darkness, thunderstruck by my sudden awareness, too full of despair even to seek the comfort of my parents' bed. What comfort can there be when there is no God?

Suddenly there was a flash of light in the room, white and brilliant as burning magnesium. I could look at it without squinting, and even more than a half-century later, I still recall the wonder of seeing light shining on my toy horse, on my plastic dolls in a row, on my cornflower-patterned wallpaper. Then I heard a young male voice say, "You wouldn't know what it is to have me unless you knew what it is to be without me. I will never leave you again."

Almost forty years went by before I told anyone about this experience, but it shaped my growing-up. From that day on I always knew that there was something behind the curtain, and surely my experience was normal. Eventually I was going to learn about it at church or in school or somewhere. I even majored in religion in college, but of course all that I learned in college was what the world's religions had taught. Since I never mentioned my experience of light, I was no closer to finding answers. By my junior year I was starting to think that I never would find answers. Then one day when I was twenty I came home from my summer job and sat down on my bed, feeling glum.

Suddenly there it was again, the magnesium-white light filling the room, this time accompanied by indescribable music. Think of a thousand tiny bells playing beautifully and loudly. Then came that same young male voice, this time saying only, "I will never leave you."

Okay Sir! I get it now!

Never for a minute since that day have I thought that I was alone, and never have I doubted the existence of God. And for many years, I was convinced that I was the literal dunce of the universe since God had to make His point to me twice. It was embarrassment more than anything else that for years led me to pray that from now on I would not forget, so He would not again need to remind me. In all the years since, He never has.

When I was in my forties, my father had a stroke. For the two weeks that he survived, I made a daily round trip to be with him. One morning I called my mother as I drove to ask how Dad had spent the night, and I found her in a state of giddiness. Something had happened that was so...

"I can't tell you! Don't ask! But it was wonderful!"

"You saw a bright light, didn't you?"

"How did you know that? How could you know that?"

"And a voice said something...?"

"How did you know that? You can't know that!"

When I got to my parents' home, I told my mother about my experiences of light. It was the first time that I had told anyone. But hearing how similar her experience was to mine, I realized that the phenomenon might be common. I began to mention my experiences of light, and I have since found that at least five percent of those with whom I have shared my experiences have had similar experiences themselves. They don't talk about them, either. It is something so personal, so extraordinary, and frankly so weird that you don't talk about it. But it is something that stays in your mind. I have no other memories from the spring of the year when I was eight, but still that predawn minute shines.

Although I had been trying to understand my experiences of light for my entire life, it was only after I learned that they had not been unique to me that my research got serious. Over the years I had assembled a little library of books on near-death experiences and other death-related topics, most with a dog-eared page at the spot where I had encountered something that seemed inconsistent with Christianity and sadly put that book down. Now eagerly I finished all those books, and they led me to other books and topics, and in turn those led me on to others. Having published novels in 1991 and 1993, I had thought briefly that I was a novelist, but after my father died I never published again. I was too busy being a lawyer and a wife and mother and spending my every spare minute reading. It wasn't long before I was able to deduce what experiences of light might be, and I dared to tie my own experiences to some that are recorded in the Bible: Moses with his burning bush; the Apostle Paul on his way to Tarsus. When there is a divine wish to get our attention, apparently experiences of light do the trick.

Most people who have experiences of light have the same sense that I did: the light is in the room, but the voice and music may be in your mind. Not that it matters. As you know having read this book, that is a distinction without much difference. The voice doesn't feel like a thought, though: you hear it clearly and externally, only not with your physical ears. Experiences of light seem to occur when we are under some spiritual strain, and not so much when we are grieving or worrying. All the messages that have been shared with me were spiritual in nature.

People differ on who it was they thought they heard speaking, and by their descriptions I have come to guess that we all hear different voices. The voice that I heard was young and male and it didn't seem quite God-like, so when in my research I encountered spirit guides, I came to think that my voice may have been my spirit guide. My mother was certain that she had heard the literal voice of God Himself, and I find it interesting that after two decades she can no longer recall her husband's post-death visit nor visits from her great-grandchildren, nor by now even what she had for lunch, but still she remembers her experience of light.

As to what makes an experience of light look and sound as it does, here are my thoughts:

- All the post-death levels exist right here, and the Summerland levels and above are filled with a white light that is brighter than sunlight. Opening a portal between our levels might leak that light through briefly, which I have come to think is what happens. It is a flash and not a flashlight.

- To hear a voice in your mind as clearly as you hear spoken words is a distinctive and remarkable experience. I think it must be very like what communication is on the post-death levels, and I assure you that you can tell the difference between spoken words and your own thoughts. No question.

Having lived successfully for decades after I had my last experience of light, having married and reared children and practiced law and made friends, I am demonstrably not crazy. But I am so glad that at the age of eight I knew enough not to tell anyone! Now I wonder how many others have been made to consider themselves insane because, like me, they had this sort of wonderful cross-dimensional message and the doctors they trusted with it decided that they had to be mad. I don't know; I just wonder. I have come to think that many things that mainstream scientists find puzzling may have their origins in the afterlife levels, which is another reason why I hope that soon they can get past their belief-based views of what reality must be.

Notes

Notes

Notes

Notes

Notes